WHERE WONDER LIVES

"*Where Wonder Lives* is one of the most intelligent, imaginative, and useful books I've seen in years. Truly, it is fun and enlightening, concrete and full of rich ideas. I have never seen deep intelligence and sensuous imagination come together so beautifully. It is practical and impractical, thought-provoking and full of charm."

~ **THOMAS MOORE,** author of *Care of the Soul*

"This is a book that speaks to the wild spaces that still live in us, longing to be awoken. It is beautiful and wise and filled with practical and powerful exercises. Every page is a seed of possibility, a glimpse at a more beautiful and vibrant future that is still within our reach. To read Fondevila's words is to forever transform the way you look at both nature and human nature."

~ **MARY REYNOLDS THOMPSON,** author of
Reclaiming the Wild Soul: How Earth's Landscapes Restore Us to Wholeness

"*Where Wonder Lives* gives us tools and potions to re-enchant our world. Fabiana Fondevila encourages us to dream with our senses—face down in the grass, reading clouds, speaking the language of birds, sipping dandelion wine. She wants us to taste our feelings and choose those that nourish the heart. She guides us through a rich imaginal geography—from swamp to mountain, from fire to ocean—in which each locale becomes a portal for adventure, soul remembering, and deepening practice. She reminds me of the most important guidance I ever received from that inner voice you learn to trust: 'Remember this world is your playground not your prison.' She invites us to make more space to play with our Magical Child and bring the joy and energy of that great imagineer into everyday life."

~ **ROBERT MOSS,** bestselling author of *Growing Big Dreams*
and *Dreaming the Soul Back Home*

"This is a special book because of the creative aliveness that leaps from every practice and every page. It is 'good company,' a vivid soul-to-soul gift of poetic textures, colors, images, and stories. This generous heart-gift shares initiations from nine sacred territories. If you accept them (in any order, by the way!), you'll keep being invited into deeper presence, joy, laughter, and wonder of wonders—this sacred and miraculous *now*-moment."

~ **TERRY PATTEN,** author of *A New Republic of the Heart* and co-author of *Integral Life Practice*

"*Where Wonder Lives* is a book you'd invite to travel the world with you. Language, myths, ideas, and clarity from many cultures and beliefs are all brought together to help us remember what is common among us in the intricate web of life. Through captivating journeys, playful practices, and researched science, Fabiana invites her readers to shift from the mirage of manageable complexity to the wonder of unmanageable simplicity. It's a book whose ideas and words can massage and reorient our innate intuition. As she quotes her own daughter, 'It's a good thing you're studying this, Mum, so I won't have to learn it from books.' What a wonder!"

~ **NIPUN MEHTA,** founder of ServiceSpace

"Wonder lives right here, in these beautifully lyrical pages that invite and entice us to play in Fabiana's magical realm and reconnect with our deepest wonder-full essence. This is a book that weaves insights from science, psychology, philosophy, myth, and the arts with playful practices that can deliver profound positive change. These pages offer an embodied and sacred experience as well as a return to the very sense of wonder that charmed you, as a child, to see not clouds but the shapes and stories they painted across the sky and deep in your heart. It is one of those books that people will not want to lend out but instead keep at hand to delve into time and time again."

~ **JANE TERESA ANDERSON,** author of *Birds of Paradise*

WHERE WONDER LIVES

Practices for
Cultivating the Sacred
in Your Daily Life

FABIANA FONDEVILA

Translated by Nick Inman

FINDHORN PRESS

Findhorn Press
One Park Street
Rochester, Vermont 05767
www.findhornpress.com

SUSTAINABLE FORESTRY INITIATIVE
Certified Sourcing
www.sfiprogram.org
SFI-00854

Text stock is SFI certified

Findhorn Press is a division of Inner Traditions International

Disclaimer
The information in this book is given in good faith and intended for
information only. Neither author nor publisher can be held liable by
any person for any loss or damage whatsoever which may arise from
the use of this book or any of the information therein.

Cataloging-in-Publication data for this title
is available from the Library of Congress

ISBN 978-1-64411-174-1 (print)
ISBN 978-1-64411-175-8 (ebook)

Printed and bound in the United States by Lake Book Manufacturing, Inc.
The text stock is SFI certified. The Sustainable Forestry Initiative® program
promotes sustainable forest management.

10 9 8 7 6 5 4 3 2 1

Edited by Jacqui Lewis
Illustrations by Maite Ortiz
Text design and layout by Anna-Kristina Larsson
This book was typeset in Garamond and Gill Sans

To send correspondence to the author of this book, mail a first-class letter
to the author c/o Inner Traditions • Bear & Company, One Park Street,
Rochester, VT 05767, USA and we will forward the communication,
or contact the author directly at **www.fabianafondevila.com**

To my father, Rafael Fondevila,
for his undying love of the world.

I will pass on the torch, Dad.

Contents

A Foreword for Those Who Skip Forewords

Have you ever noticed that different books require different ways of moving through them? There are books for pedestrians and books for sprinters. There are books that make you walk slowly through them, as if you were ambling in a park, and others that simply invite you to swing in an imaginary hammock, even while you are reading them on the subway at rush hour.

Where Wonder Lives is a book for dancers. If you like dancing, you will dance through its pages; and if you need to learn a dancing way of reading you couldn't find a more gifted instructor than Fabiana Fondevila.

Like all the best teachers, the author guides her students in a playful way. Almost without noticing it, you will pick up valuable insights from meetings with psychologists, anthropologists, biologists and other masters of their arts; and you will encounter great poets. But the learning process will be different from that which you experienced at school. Instead, you will rediscover the art of serious play, an art we perfected as children but which, alas, our schools un-taught us. Even for someone who had the best schooling, the saying is valid: "Childhood is too short for us to become the children we are meant to be."

But it is not too late. Every ritual offers your inner child a form of play with purpose and meaning, and this book will teach you how to turn the simple actions of daily living into rituals. To the extent to which you master the art of celebrating every moment in this way, you learn to tap the deepest meaning of life.

As you start to read this book, be prepared to go on a journey that is different from any other journey you have ever made. On this journey you will not walk, or ride, or fly—you will dance. Wonderment makes us dance, dance as we would at a wedding—the sacred wedding between our *animus*, which ascends into the realms of reason, and our *anima*, which descends into feelings. The steps of the dance lead you into exercises that may turn out to be the most enjoyable and at the same time the most transformative parts of the book. "We are perishing for lack of wonder," wrote G. K. Chesterton. But we need not perish. In today's torrent of disenchantment, a book that teaches us where wonderment lives hands us a lifebelt.

Brother David Steindl-Rast
Order of Saint Benedict
The Feast of Candlemas, 2 February 2018

David Steindl-Rast studied arts, anthropology and psychology, and was one of the first Catholics to receive training in Zen Buddhism. He is a specialist in inter-religious dialogue; a speaker; and the author of a dozen books. His video *A Good Day* has been admired around the world for its call to live a life of wonder and gratitude. **www.gratefulness.org**

Instructions for living a life:
Pay attention.
Be astonished.
Tell about it.

Mary Oliver

A stylistic clarification. In English an author is obliged to specify gender when using the third person singular pronoun (either he or she). Rather than use one or the other consistently throughout, I have deliberately alternated between the two. Except for where the context makes clear otherwise, I am always referring to a human being of any gender identity.

Introduction

I was about eight years old. My parents had bought a plot of land on the outskirts of Buenos Aires, in an area that someone had once named, with more romanticism than sense of reality, "The Hills." We went every weekend—except when there was a storm—to plant trees and vegetables, dig ditches and pretend we had a home there, out among the birds and the trees.

As soon as my dad parked the Renault on the grassy track, my brothers and I would jump on the gate like a bride throwing herself into the arms of her beloved. The gate swung open . . . and off we went! I don't know how far my brothers got, but I ran until I was out of breath and the opposite fence, an ocean of grass away, was almost within reach. The smell of dry earth, the tall weeds that brushed my nose, the space that opened up in all directions—more space than an indoor city girl had ever seen—made me drunk with joy. The buzz lasted all afternoon, throughout the trip back, and until it was time to go back to school.

No house was ever built on that plot, as my father had dreamt. Never a modest dreamer, he actually envisioned five houses: one in the center, for his retirement years with my mother; and four around it for us, his children. There never was a house; but there were pumpkins, melons, watermelons, an avenue of eucalyptus, a cement shed and a seemingly endless hosepipe. And, for me, a niggling in my soul that would only make sense decades later, when I finally tackled questions that I heard whispered in my ear back then: questions about the nature of my connection with the world; questions of kinship; questions of belonging.

Those country adventures travel with me still, as a kind of traveling altar. Fortunately this only exists in my imagination. If it existed in the material world, it would have turned yellow long ago, and in any case, there would be no shelf or chest capable of holding everything associated with it. Perhaps it is more than an altar; it is an ongoing nature journal in which new discoveries and wonderments are inscribed each day. Its pages contain the daily gestures (minute or extraordinary) of the people I love; colors (the turquoise of the sky on certain summer days, the coral buds of early spring, the deep indigo of morning glory flowers when the sun comes up, the black filigree of treetops in the dusk); textures (fur, skin, wood), aromas (linden trees in the shade, pines in the sunshine), astonishments (the Milky Way, the music of certain poems, the kindness of some people); love in its myriad gradations.

All this is part of my personal pantheon, the ever-growing reservoir that honors and celebrates everything I hold sacred. I am aware of the halo of solemnity that surrounds the word "sacred." I use it with the intention of redefining it in a more humble and earthy manner.

Originally, "the sacred" was what took place within the walls of the church, while "the profane" was what happened beyond its threshold. In the vision that I propose in these pages, nothing could really be outside the orbit of the sacred, because it is not a place or an object, but a way of looking at life, a way of feeling the world.

Like the poet and naturalist theologian Thomas Berry, I feel that "there are no sacred places and profane places; there are sacred places and desecrated places." If the sacred is in the eyes that perceive love and mystery at the heart of life, then desecrating means ignoring or violating that love and that mystery; ignoring or violating the bonds that unite us. "Profane" is cynicism, denigration, humiliation, contempt. And, it must be said, this is not the exclusive terrain of a few bestial beings. We can all, unwittingly, commit desecration when we act with cruelty out of fear; with resentment due to confusion; or with coldness or apathy because we cannot tolerate a difficult emotion.

The practices offered in these pages seek to restore the qualities of the heart that help us to see, appreciate and celebrate the sacred in the small events of each day and, through them, life itself. All are born of the same intuition: that if mystery exists, it is present in the anthill in the same measure as in the snowy peak; that love is our true nature, no matter how richly or poorly we express it at any given moment; that, if we are an amalgam of spirit and matter, one must necessarily embrace the other, as the coal of night gives way to the glow of daylight.

This is the journey that I propose to take you on: one that will open your eyes wide; cause your ears to prick up; sharpen your sense of smell; invite you to take a long deep breath. To explore your life with the boldness of a seafarer; to go mad with love for the wild and phenomenal world; and, at the end of the day, like a good-hearted pirate, to give back the treasure that you set off to find.

TWO PATHS DIVERGE

From the beginning, human beings have sought to understand the laws that govern the universe, their role in the great cosmic orchestra and the meaning of an existence marked by the constant interplay of joy and pain, beauty and abomination, amazement and anguish, life and death.

Early on, this search for meaning led humanity to explore the spiritual dimension. This exploration took two main paths, following the two movements described by Plato and the Neo-Platonists: an ascending directionality, which follows matter to spirit; and a descending path, which goes from spirit to matter. According to this vision, the cosmos is a multidimensional whole, composed of ascending and descending currents of divine love.

The people and traditions that adopted the ascending course—the monotheistic religions (with notable exceptions, such as the mystic Saint Francis of Assisi)—sought spirit in the lofty heights of existence and prioritized "masculine" values and aspirations such as pure light, vision and the transcendent. Through prayers, fasts, meditations and austere lifestyles, these traditions sought to leave behind the imperfect world of form to focus on the eternal source of everything that exists.

On the other hand, the people who adopted the descending vision—the pagan, shamanic, predominantly matriarchal cultures—found the divine reflected in every leaf and creature. They cultivated feminine values, privileging what binds us together, the earthly and the immanent. Rather than aspiring to enlightenment, these people delved into the underworld, which is the realm of the soul.

What is the soul in this conception? It is the primitive and essential core of our individuality, the portion of spirit that lives in us and adopts our peculiar characteristics—those that distinguish us from all others.

The descending journey plunges into the depths, in search of that particular expression of the sacred that is you. It explores our animal nature, our deepest fears, our dialogue with death and disease, our experience of sexuality, our desires, our creations, our dreams, our unconscious and its symbols.

This is how the brilliant Jungian psychologist James Hillman defines the difference between spirit and soul:

> Soul likes intimacy, spirit is uplifting. Soul gets hairy; spirit is bald. Spirit sees, even in the dark; soul feels its way, step by step, or needs a dog. Spirit shoots arrows, soul takes them in the chest. William James and D. H. Lawrence said it best. Spirit likes wholes. Souls like eaches.

In his book *Soulcraft: Crossing into the Mysteries of Nature and Psyche*, depth psychologist and wilderness guide Bill Plotkin gives a more formal definition:

> Where soul is associated with the many earthly mysteries, spirit is associated with the one heavenly bliss. Soul opens the door to the unknown or the not-yet-known, while spirit is the realm of beyond knowledge of any kind, consciousness without an object. Soul is encountered in the subconscious (i.e., that which lies below awareness), while spirit is apprehended in states of super-consciousness. Both are associated with states of ecstasy (i.e., outside the ordinary), but the encounter with soul is characterized by dreams and visions of personal destiny, while spirit realization engenders pure, content-free awareness.

The two paths—ascending and descending—complement and complete each other. Each, in itself, offers a partial experience of the divine. However, since the advent of modernity the downward path has been discouraged, if not downright forbidden. Says Plotkin, again:

> Perhaps our religious and political forefathers were afraid of the influences of nature and soul, steered us away from the wild, and tried to control or destroy wildness wherever it might be found. Fear of nature and soul is a fear of our own essence.

Through this split vision, the Earth and its creatures lost their divine status. The schism worsened in the 18th century, with the advent of rationalism. Without wanting to minimize the progress brought by this stage of development, it also appointed the intellect as the new divinity and dismissed all other forms of knowledge as mere superstition. The wisdom of indigenous peoples, based on intuition and dialogue with the forces of nature, was denied, or attributed to an infantile stage of human consciousness.

The myth of unlimited scientific and industrial progress, with its view of nature as a resource to be exploited, became dominant and today threatens to destroy the planet. The rejection of matter—first from a spiritual standpoint, then an intellectual one—gave way, paradoxically, to an age of unprecedented materialism.

This change of outlook impoverished our experience of the world: we lost the capacity to dialogue with other species, to recognize ourselves in the rhythms and cycles of nature, to feel comfortable in our bodies and with the bodies of others; in short, *to belong*.

In the second half of the 20th century, the New Age movement brought winds of change, espousing an environmental, feminist, libertarian and progressive agenda. It was a necessary turning point, fueled in part by the influence of Eastern wisdom reaching the West, and the meeting of two worlds. However, over the decades it ended up feeding the antagonism, by prioritizing transcendence as the only way to access spirit. One of the most visible results of this preference is the phenomenon that the author Robert Augustus Masters has baptized "spiritual bypassing": the propensity to want to solve physical or psychological problems solely by resorting to spiritual (meditative, contemplative, energetic) practices; that is, using these practices as if they were shortcuts to healing. Those who fall into this confusion can avoid consulting a medical professional for serious physical symptoms; repress emotions such as anger or fear because they consider them "unspiritual"; endure abuse in the name of a misunderstood "compassion"; or avoid difficult but important conversations for the sake of maintaining peace.

Another aspect of the same phenomenon is what Buddhist teacher Chögyam Trungpa named "spiritual materialism": the use of spirituality to achieve personal goals in the world, which ultimately denaturalizes it.

Authors such as Ken Wilber, founder of integral thinking, warn that decades of Buddhist practices for building detachment and equanimity have done little to foster the psychological and emotional maturity of practitioners. In other words, no matter how hard someone strives for peace and discipline in the dojo, temple or weekend retreat, if they do not work actively to solve their work, family or personal problems, if they do not examine their shadows and take care of the mundane details of their existence, then their efforts in pursuit of enlightenment will be in vain. Proof of this is provided by the scandals that shook the North American Buddhist community when gurus from remote monasteries, who had had little or no contact with money, women or sexuality, arrived in the United States and found themselves surrounded by a world of unknown temptations. Is it any wonder they committed adolescent blunders, and even erred into abuse? Wilber cautions: it is not enough to wake up; it is also necessary to grow up.

Thomas Moore, author of the best-seller *Care of the Soul*, also distrusts a spirituality that only favors transcendence at the expense of the earthly:

> If we define our spirituality only in positive and glowing terms, it will become sentimental, and then it is of no use. To be spiritual is not just to pray and meditate but also to be involved in the struggles of marriage, work, and raising children; in social responsibility and in the effort to make a just and peaceful world.

In this worldview, "spiritual activism" is not a contradiction in terms but a concrete expression of love in action.

The truth is that we need both: the ascending path, which seeks the source through vision, wisdom and detachment; and the descending path, that finds the divine here on Earth and strives to express it through service, generosity and compassion.

In our lives, we naturally move from one polarity to the other: we seek out silence in search of inspiration and contentment; then we return to the world and share that peace with our community. Or, conversely: we experience some mundane event—a friend who offers help; a sky strewn with stars; a bird that feeds its young—and that propels us straight into the mystery.

We need to embrace the multidimensionality of life: to match light with shadow; being with doing; giving with receiving; spiritual elevation with psychological and emotional maturation. Recovering the feminine face of the sacred is a way to correct the imbalance and give the world the food for which it has longed for centuries: the sacred marriage that integrates opposites and brings us integrity. That very same longing inspires these pages.

A MAP OF THE JOURNEY

Human beings are makers of meaning by nature. Just as we learned to procure our own sustenance, protect ourselves from the cold and to build shelter, with equal determination we searched the stars for the reason behind our feelings, perceived symbols in the flames and intuitively understood that the trees, the waters and the sky were living beings, just like us. We asked the mountains for protection, performed rites of atonement by spilling the blood of our prey, sang the moon's praises and celebrated the return of the sun.

Today we live infinitely safer and more comfortable lives than we did in early times, but we have lost something of the simple charm that the world held for our ancestors. Can we recover the vitality of that belonging? Can we rediscover, in the creatures and the landscape, the reflections of our inner experience? Can we once again feel intimately connected (without too much intellectual interference) with other people; with the cosmos and life itself? Joseph Campbell, the great mythologist, alluded to this deep yearning when he said:

> People say that what we're all seeking is a meaning for life. I don't think
> that's what we're really seeking. I think that what we're seeking is an
> experience of being alive, so that our life experiences on the purely
> physical plane will have resonances with our own innermost being and
> reality, so that we actually feel the rapture of being alive.

This book proposes a way back to that intimacy. Or, rather, nine ways. Nine steps across an imaginary map that invite you to go where you have never been; pick up where you left off; or simply rekindle the joy of being here, conscious and in good company, on this green-blue orb turning slowly through space.

It is a map, and not an itinerary, because it does not propose a linear route. You can enter this territory where you want—the part that is closest to you, the landscape that seduces you, the habitat you need—and create your journey organically according to your time and circumstances. What are the territories, or stages, of the map? They are dimensions of life worth exploring; topographies in which human beings have found joy, peace and fulfillment since the beginning of time.

The Jungle

the Garden

the Village

the Fire

The division between these stages is, of course, arbitrary, since in life everything is connected by a thousand and one threads, visible and invisible. But there is value in stopping to admire each facet of the prism and wander through it, in the same way as someone who visits a planet for the first time takes note of everything he or she sees, hears and feels. Every exploration is, in a way, just a scouting of the terrain, since each station is a world in itself and will certainly deserve longer and more exhaustive visits. If you want to investigate further, at the end of the book you will find the names of travelers who have laid the groundwork for you. Or, of course, you may decide to make other journeys, guided by different compasses. The purpose of this map will have been fulfilled if, after a visit to any of the territories I describe, you leave with a desire to return.

In addition to describing the terrain, each stage includes practical activities or exercises, and it is here—in exploring these activities—where any value this book may have lies. An exercise is nothing more than self-directed learning, in which the focus is not on reaching some destination but on the intrinsic value of the path, and the intention with which you travel. Just as meditating is, in some way, waking up every time you find yourself distracted from your objective (observing your breath, for example), and gently returning to it, all practice is an invitation to return, again and again, to what we set out to do. It is the act of returning, that constant renewal of vows, that feeds slow and unsuspected transformations. As Rumi advises, his wisdom echoing through the centuries:

> Submit to a daily practice.
> Your loyalty to that is a ring on the door.
> Keep knocking and the joy inside
> will eventually open a window
> and look out to see who's there.

You can travel the road alone, at your own pace, stopping where something inspires you to investigate more thoroughly. But it is a good idea to be accompanied by a guide, therapist or spiritual teacher, a friend or, better yet, a *sangha* (a community of peers, in the Buddhist tradition). One reason for this is that some of the practices are intense and can trigger emotions and experiences that require loving containment. Another is that collective intelligence strengthens any process, resulting in greater understanding and growth for all involved. A journey undertaken on your own can be a beautiful challenge; the same path traveled in the company of other brave souls becomes an adventure. These are the territories we will explore:

1 The Jungle
In this realm we commune with wild nature. What we were, what we are, what we are made of. In this stage you will learn to make your own herbal medicine, decipher the language of birds, learn the geography of the sky. With this knowledge you can begin to recover your place in the primordial fabric of life, or, even better, to realize that you never really left it.

2 The Garden
Seeing, hearing, smelling, tasting, touching: a world of sensations awaits you in the garden. The gift of your five senses, and others you may not even know about, can open the door to a greater intimacy with the world, and other beings, if you only stop to experience them. The secret garden is only secret until you discover it.

3 The River
Its waters circle around stones, rise in waves and sweep you off your feet. This magical flying carpet is the land of imagination and that is what we cover here. This faculty transports you back to childhood; it allows you to reinvent the world and to discover it in unusual ways. What wonders does the universe hold for you when you explore it with your eyes closed?

4 The Mountaintop
Here, among the snowy peaks and in the pristine air, you can look at your life from a mythical viewpoint and discover that the road you have traveled is much more than the sum of random events. From the peak, you will see even the most arduous of your problems as just another figure in a shadow theater show. The view from the top does not erase the effort of the climb: it rewards it.

5 The Swamp
Every now and then in life you run into quicksand. The ground gives way under your feet and you find yourself stuck: you are in the swamp, face to face with your own shadow. Light doesn't shine in this corner of your kingdom, much as you would like it to. But the swamp is

daunting only in appearance. If you stop fighting it, it will surprise you with its fertility and hidden, life-renewing treasures.

6 The Village

It is here that we meet to chat, to buy and sell our harvests, to seal pacts and negotiations, to fight, to make amends. And it is here, in the shelter of your connections with others, where your greatest happiness and your greatest misfortune play out. In this realm, you will explore practices to turn your relationships—even the most challenging ones, particularly the most challenging ones—into a path of growth.

7 The Fire

We seek the fire pit at night, driven by some important event. Around its flame we mourn our departed, celebrate our victories, sing to our deities and seek their guidance and comfort. By performing rites and ceremonies, humans seek to make the invisible visible and to proclaim as sacred that which we treasure most, so that not even the gods can look the other way.

8 The Lighthouse

Life is full of demands and distractions, and the mind follows them all like a restless dog. In this station you will learn practices to calm and focus the mind, resorting to the guiding light of consciousness to return you to the only place that is truly safe: the present moment, in which life happens.

9 The Ocean

It all starts and ends here, in the deep waters of the heart. This is the birthplace of the emotions that transcend our differences: awe, gratitude, joy, forgiveness, kindness, compassion. In this stage we will nurture openness, radical affirmation and the courage to feel it all, anchored in the deep and abiding power of love.

THE JUNGLE
Re-wild Yourself

I come into the presence of still water.
And I feel above me the day-blind stars
waiting with their light. For a time
I rest in the grace of the world, and am free.
Wendell Berry

To climb these coming crests
one word to you, to
you and your children:
stay together
learn the flowers
step lightly.
Gary Snyder

Remember the Earth whose skin you are.
Joy Harjo

We walk among the broad leaves, the translucent ferns, the vines. Hummingbirds stir the air, sowing the pollen path with their wings. An emerald parrot pecks the pulp of a mango. Bees buzz. Butterflies rest in the sun. There are coconuts in the palm trees; bananas in the banana trees; a cool mist arises from a waterfall. Are we in paradise? Indeed we are: we are on Earth!

Perhaps not all habitats are as exuberant as the jungle, but each offers its peculiar richness and beauty, as well as some form of sustenance that has fed and delighted human beings since the beginning of time. We grow and live here, like the coconuts and the bananas, the bees and the hummingbirds, and nothing that happens on this planet is foreign to us. We seem to have forgotten this fact, and how to act accordingly.

The Potawatomi Indians, of the great prairies of North America, tell a creation story. One day, the Sky Woman fell towards the great sea holding a handful of seeds. During her fall, she suddenly felt the brush of feathers under her body: it was a flock of geese that had gathered to catch her. But they could not hold her for long, and they were going to hit the water. The geese called a council of animals to meet beneath the woman. A turtle offered the curve of its back for her to rest on. Several animals remembered having seen mud at the bottom of the ocean and they decided to look for it. They knew the woman would need land to cultivate and to live on.

One after the other, the duck, the otter, the beaver and the sturgeon went down, without success. Finally, the muskrat offered to go. Nobody thought he would manage it. It was a long time before he returned. At last, they saw a necklace of bubbles rise out of the water and, below it, the lifeless body of the muskrat. Someone noticed that his paw was closed. What was he holding there? A little ball of mud. He had given his life to save the woman.

The turtle said: "Put the mud ball on my back," and so they did. Gratefully, the Sky Woman began to sing. As she sang, the earth began to grow around her. They called it Turtle Island. But the Sky Woman had not come empty-handed. As she fell she had reached out to some branches of the tree of life and had brought fruits and seeds from it in her hand. She scattered the seeds on the earth, and from them flowers, wild grass, trees and plants of all kinds were born. And, now that there was room, many animals joined the woman on Turtle Island.

This is the story told by Robin Wall Kimmerer, descendant of the Potawatomi people, in her book *Braiding Sweetgrass: Indigenous Wisdom, Scientific Knowledge and the Teachings of Plants.*

But we also know the story of another woman in another garden, and a different set of events. Far from receiving the help of animals and collaborating to create the Earth together, in the Judeo-Christian origin myth, Eve is tempted by the serpent to taste the forbidden fruit. That gesture of intimacy with the Earth results in her exile. From then on, she and her partner must earn their living with the sweat of their brow, forever estranged from the abundant universe that was once their home. Our creation myths shape us much more deeply than we suspect. As the heirs of Adam and Eve, we live isolated from creation, divorced from paradise. It's time for us to tell ourselves a better story.

RE-INHABITING THE WORLD

The plants that grow out of pavements have a history longer than our own. Birds communicate their news in songs and calls. Insects tunnel their way through the earth. The clouds draw the geography of the sky and the stars speak the language of light. We are surrounded by a living and vibrant universe that we barely know, and that we rarely feel as our own.

On any given day, you may connect with nature at some random moment. Perhaps you take a quick look at the sky, admire the moon when it draws a perfect arabesque in the darkness, or stop to admire some blooms on a flower stall. On holiday, you may allow yourself to live a fleeting love affair with the sea, a river, or the green silence of a hillside. But, if we are honest, most of us think of nature more as a place to visit than, as naturalist poet Gary Snyder proposes, as our one and only home.

What is nature, exactly? We could start with a definition of what it is **not**:

- The distant landscape that we spy through the window, on our way somewhere. It is not something "out there." It is not an idea or a horizon. It is not an "other."

- It is not Neverland (the imaginary country that gave Peter Pan and his friends the gift of eternal childhood). It is neither bucolic nor perfect.
- It is not cruel, bloody or completely unpredictable.
- It is not a resource designed to meet human needs. In the words of Thomas Berry, "The world is not a collection of objects, but a community of subjects."
- It is not "the only thing that is real" while everything created by human beings is "false" or "artificial."

It is not easy to give a positive, precise and complete definition of a reality so wide and so foundational, but perhaps we come close when we say that nature is the vital and primal force that inhabits us at every moment, feeding us and keeping us alive. We are nature and we are it all the time, no matter how far away or how close we perceive it to be at each moment. We are nature, even if we find ourselves enclosed by concrete walls, without a window or even a stamp-size view of the sky. You might even say that the lamp and the bed and the slippers underneath it, and even your computer, are "secondary nature" (as some authors have dubbed it), because we cannot create anything that is not built with its raw materials.

How exactly do we find nature in ourselves? Kathleen Dean Moore, a professor of moral philosophy and philosophy of nature, put it this way in a conversation we shared about the concept of "the wild": "It's in the light that warms our skin, in the air we breathe, in the water that we drink, in the iron in our blood. We are made of earth and the Earth is made of stars. I think this makes us creatures of nature."

This being so, can anything cut us off from this connection? "Nothing can suppress the wild in us. But we can lose our awareness of our connection to it. And this is a major loss," says Dean Moore.

Nothing can separate us from this relationship, because our relationships define us, even from the biological point of view. So says David Haskell, a professor of biology at the University of Tennessee and author of *The Songs of Trees*:

We are all—trees, humans, insects, birds, bacteria—pluralities.
Life is an embodied network. These living systems are not places of benevolent oneness. Instead, they are places where the ecological and evolutionary tensions between cooperation and conflict are negotiated and resolved. These struggles often end not in the evolution of stronger

and disconnected individuals, but in the dissolution of the individual in the bond.

Since life is a network, there is no "nature" or "environment" separate from humans, emphasizes Haskell, nor are we the "fallen" beings of nature, as romantic poets such as William Blake suggested. "Our bodies and our minds, 'our science and our art,' are as natural and wild as they always were," Haskell assures.

Children though we are of the Earth and the stars, we created an ambitious culture that eventually convinced us of our own autonomy. We feel and act like powerful, superior, self-sufficient beings. Our interaction with the planet is increasingly like that of a feudal lord towards a serf: we give it crumbs of our attention, and in return we ask for its full subservience.

This vision not only exhausts the planet's resources, it also erodes our souls. The link between nature and the soul is evident even in language. Bill Plotkin, guide of shamanic vision quests, points out that the word "nature" comes from *natus*, "being born," and that "the nature" of a thing is "the dynamic principle that holds it together and gives it identity." In other words, it is the essence. "Since the human soul is the essential core of our nature, then, when we are guided by the soul, we are guided by nature," says Plotkin. Is there anything we can do to restore this link? Do we still have time to re-establish our kinship?

Indeed we do. We may live in brick houses; we may move around in metal boxes; but the smell of the earth finds us wherever we go. The poet— and farmer—Wendell Berry says, "The earth under the grass dreams of a young forest, and under the pavement the earth dreams of grass." We can satisfy our longing: we can renew our belonging. Let us count the ways.

EATING THE WILD

They grow in all corners: at the base of trees, in the daintiest flowerbeds, in the cracks of the pavements. We pass them by unknowingly. If someone asked about their name or identity, the answer would most likely be: "Oh that? That's just a weed!"

What is a weed, exactly? Naturalist writer and philosopher Ralph Waldo Emerson defined it thus: "A weed is a plant that grows where we do not want it." On the other hand, Michael Pollan, author of *Second Nature: A Gardener's Education*, thinks a weed is a plant with a peculiar character. Weeds camouflage themselves skillfully among crops; they know how to adapt to almost any climatic condition; and they have learned to outsmart most pests and pesticides. And one more thing: they follow human beings around like their shadow.

These vilified botanical beings rear up their heads wherever dirt has been disturbed. In other words: they are the offspring of civilization. They do not proliferate so much in virgin forests, deserts or prairies as in wastelands and fields, on tracks and at roadsides.

They no longer belong to particular regions: they are cosmopolitan. From the beginning, they moved with us in our backpacks, in our pockets and on the soles of our shoes. Today they are citizens of the world and thrive among brick walls and granite citadels.

Perhaps because they have evolved with us, weeds are abundant, infinitely adaptable, and have endless virtues to offer us: they contain a greater amount of vitamins and minerals than most vegetables we buy in the supermarket, and many have medicinal properties. That is why the Argentinian researcher Eduardo Rapoport, emeritus professor at the University of Comahue, reclassified them as "beneficial" and devoted much of his life to the noble task of teaching schoolchildren in poor areas of Patagonia how to recognize them, harvest them, and make them into everyday meals.

None of this was new to our great-grandparents, who lived off these plants, using them for food, medicine, materials and shelter (as well as extracting dyes to color their clothes and decorate their homes). Today we walk past them or exterminate them because they annoy us, interfere with our garden designs or compete with our crops. We do not know their names or their properties, and we would not even think of serving them at table.

Herbalist and author Stephen Harrod Buhner has a provocative explanation for this reticence:

Our mothers intuitively understood something essential: the green is poisonous to civilization. If we eat the wild, it begins to work inside us, altering us, changing us. Soon, if we eat too much, we will no longer fit the suit that has been made for us. Our hair will begin to grow long and ragged. Our gait and how we hold our body will change. A wild light begins to gleam in our eyes. Our words start to sound strange, nonlinear, emotional. Unpractical. Poetic.

Once we have tasted this wildness, we begin to hunger for a food long denied us, and the more we eat of it the more we will awaken.

It is no wonder that we are taught to close off our senses to Nature. Through these channels, the green paws of Nature enter into us, climb over us, search within us, find all our hiding places, burst us open, and blind the intellectual eye with hanging tendrils of green.

The terror is an illusion, of course. For most of our million years on this planet, human beings have daily eaten the wild. It's just that the linear mind knows what will happen if you eat it now.

What will happen? Little by little, you will recover forgotten aspects of your psyche, aspects that do not always fit in nicely with the decorum that society expects of us. The wildness in us is frightening because we imagine it to be ungovernable. So we repress it, splitting off an essential part of our being. "To speak of wildness is to speak of wholeness," says poet and ecologist Gary Snyder, "Human beings emerged out of that wholeness."

Henry David Thoreau (1817–1862) was another pioneer of the "re-wildness" movement. The American writer spent two years, two months and two days living in a small, humble cabin he built himself in a forest in Concord, Massachusetts, near Walden Pond (which provided the title for the essay in which he would narrate the experience: *Walden; or, Life in the Woods*). His intention was to prove for himself, and demonstrate to the world, that life in nature is the best (or possibly, the only) life for a free man. "I went to the woods because I wished to live deliberately. To front only the essential facts of life. And see if I could not learn what it had to teach and not, when I came to die, discover that I had not lived," he wrote. These words, carved in wood, welcome tourists and visitors who go to his forest today, even though the wildness itself is mostly a memory.

Thoreau belonged to the group of poets and philosophers known as transcendentalists, who emerged in the early 19th century on the east coast of the United States. Influenced by English and German Romanticism, Hinduism and other traditions, these thinkers spoke out against the excess of intellectualism and the puritanical religious views of the time, defending the essential goodness of man and nature and advocating a return to a simple and essential lifestyle. This is how Thoreau described it:

Nature is not, of course, always benign and beautiful. It can be frightening and terrifying also. Not too many generations ago, raw nature and wilderness tended to inspire fear and dread in "civilized" people. They represented Otherness and the Unknown. That which is "wild" is also "bewildering." Today, wilderness is usually considered to be something good and in need of preservation. The beauty and awesomeness of it dominate our attention. We are attracted by wilderness, the Otherness of it, the sense it is something inevitably outside of us. Always beyond us, it is what is ultimately real. We cannot adequately appreciate this aspect of nature if we approach it with any taint of human pretense. It will elude us if we allow artifacts like clothing to intervene between ourselves and this Other. To apprehend it, we cannot be naked enough. In Wildness is the preservation of the world.

Can we recover the totality of who we are? We can start by eating wild plants, as we once did.

Let's look at the first concern that arises when considering this proposal: can the wild kill us? This was the fear behind the question I asked the American herbalist Susun Weed many years ago, at the beginning of my own research: "Is it dangerous to eat wild plants?" Her response was blunt: "Life is dangerous."

It was not an ironic or evasive answer, merely empirical. Of course there are plants whose content of alkaloids and other compounds makes them toxic to humans. But it is also true that a wide variety of wild plants have been consumed as food or used as medicine for millennia. Much longer than most of the processed foods and synthetic medicines that make up our daily menu and our first-aid kit. In fact, the rate of consultations for poisoning is infinitely higher for allopathic drugs than for herbs of any kind.

Safety resides in education and knowledge: reading; researching on reliable websites and plant identification forums; and slow, careful experimentation. Toxic plants usually have some distinguishing feature: a foul-smelling aroma, unpleasant taste, shiny leaves. But this is not an infallible method. The best way to protect yourself is to learn from an experienced herbalist who has been consuming wild plants for at least a couple of years. In the past, the fact that this knowledge was transmitted from generation to generation (knowledge of the properties of plants as well as recipes and ways to use them) minimized the risks considerably.

I remember one day when my daughter found me buried in a pile of botanical tomes and said, "It's good that you're studying all this, Mum, so I won't have to learn it from books." There is nothing like recognizing plants *in situ*; touching them; smelling them and becoming familiar with the stages of their lifecycles.

That said, if you ever find yourself in a survival situation and you have to eat a plant you can't identify with certainty, the best way to avoid intoxication is to ingest a tiny portion of leaf or fruit—approximately a centimeter square—and wait two hours. If there is no stomach discomfort or other adverse symptom, you can try another piece of the same size. Two hours later, repeat the operation, and so on until you feel sure that you have suffered no ill effects. Always try plants one by one.

Another reason we reject some wild plants is the bitter taste that many of them have. It is important to deal with this aversion because the bitter taste has medicinal effects: it stimulates digestive secretions; tones the liver; improves metabolism; and helps repair mucosal damage. Some experts ascribe emotional and even spiritual virtues to this taste. For American herbalist Jim McDonald, bitter brings us back to the present by lowering the energy from the head to the viscera; and the English herbalist Sara Head suggests that this little-known taste in our diet mobilizes emotions stuck in the body.

For all these reasons, it is advisable to eat a salad with bitter leaves seasoned with vinegar before meals: bitter herbs help prepare your body for digestion, and vinegar helps to extract the minerals they possess and to make them available.

Another objection often raised by those who oppose the consumption of wild plants is hygiene. It is advisable to avoid harvesting areas frequented by animals, or where there are streets or highways nearby. Putting the leaves or harvested roots in water with a few tablespoons of apple cider vinegar for a while will kill a lot of germs and dangerous bacteria. It should be added that the fruits and vegetables we eat every day are sprayed with pesticides, which are no less risky in the long run than any contaminants on a wild plant.

An interesting fact: archeo-botanical investigations reveal that the more aggressive a plant is in its territorial expansion, the more edible it is. You will do well to pay attention to plants that multiply "like the plague" in your neighborhood. Sometimes the same force used by a species to conquer territories is also expressed in the power of its nutrients.

How to Supply Yourself with Plants

There is a very simple way to acquire plants for a "weed garden": leave some bare soil in any pot or piece of garden, and sit around and wait. You will have the unusual pleasure of discovering the mysteries that will sprout seasonally, one after the other, in your little homemade herbarium.

Another way is to collect plants that interest you from where they grow and transplant them into a pot, or put them in a patch of earth. You can live with them while they acclimatize to their new surroundings, observing them closely and learning their habits and how they grow. "Anything will give up its secrets if you love it enough," said the theologian George Washington Carver.

When you go out to harvest weeds, you need take only a few items. A basic collecting kit: scissors or secateurs, a trowel (in case you want to bring a specimen home with its roots) and a basket or some paper bags.

You will also need to adjust your inner compass. We are used to sailing distractedly along above the ground, prisoners of some thought or busy exchanging messages through a screen. A weed walk is an adventure of immersion. You have to go slowly, counteracting your tendency to notice only the big, the colorful, the outstanding. Wild plants are usually short (they are often cut before they have a chance to develop); they do not have spectacular shapes; and they tend to be camouflaged among the grass and other plants. You have to go slowly, attentively, with your senses and curiosity on high alert.

Dandelion

Most importantly, always take only what you need, leave a "grandmother plant" to continue seeding the area and to feed insects and critters, and remember to give thanks for everything you take.

Why don't you join me on a virtual weed walk? Get your basket and let's go!

Dandelion

(Taraxacum officinale)

It's a nice spring day, perfect for venturing out into the street or the nearest park. The first stop is nearby. All you have to do is choose any corner, lower your gaze or kneel down, and look around you. You can bet that within one or two meters of your chosen place you will see the toothed and shiny leaves of the dandelion.

This small, humble plant, usually recognized by its yellow flowers and its fluffy seed heads or "clocks," has a vitality that has great health-giving properties but also makes it the number one enemy of farmers.

It is edible from end to end: leaves, flowers and roots. The leaves can be eaten raw in salads, but if you find the bitter taste off-putting, boil them twice for a minute, changing the water each time, and then macerate them with honey and soy sauce, or sauté them with olive oil and garlic. What nutrients do they supply? Vitamins A, B and C; potassium, iron, calcium, manganese, phosphorus, magnesium, carotene.

The flowers are extremely versatile. They can be used to make cookies, puddings, honey, pancakes, or the famous dandelion wine immortalized by Ray Bradbury in his semi-autobiographical novel of the same name: a yellow-colored liqueur that captures the essence of summer to drink all year round. Finally, the toasted root is an excellent coffee substitute.

In its curative aspect it is a good example of "broad-spectrum medicine," being at once a digestive, a stimulant to bile flow, an aperitif and a restorative. It is also a diuretic of excellence, since—unlike most synthetic diuretics—it does not steal potassium from the organism, but supplies it.

As if all this isn't enough, an infusion made from the flowers cleanses and purifies the skin and can soothe everything from mild skin irritations to scratches and acne.

And that's not all: the whole plant can be used to make dandelion fertilizer to stimulate the growth of other plants.

DANDELION FLOWER PANCAKES

4 cups freshly harvested and washed flowers
2 cups flour
2 eggs
2 cups milk

- Pour the milk into a bowl with the flour and eggs and mix well to make a batter.
- Remove the sepals (the green parts that join the petals together); these are very slightly bitter. Add the flowers to the mixture. The petals will fall apart when you remove the sepals.
- Heat a little butter in a frying pan. Pour in a tablespoon of batter; let it cook and then turn the pancake until it is golden brown on both sides. It should look like an American pancake, somewhat thicker than other kinds.
- Transfer to a plate spread with a sheet of kitchen paper to absorb the excess butter.

The pancakes can be eaten as they are or with honey. They can also be sprinkled with icing sugar or flavored with cinnamon, ginger or any other spice you fancy.

DANDELION ROOT COFFEE

- Collect the roots of at least four plants, preferably in the autumn (which is when the nutrients are most concentrated).
- Chop them up and wash them well.
- Roast them in the oven, or toast them in a frying pan on a low heat, until they start giving off a rich toasted aroma.
- Keep them in a paper bag or jar.

To make the coffee, boil the roots for ten minutes (or until the water turns the color of coffee). Sweeten to taste with sugar or honey.

DANDELION FLOWER JAM

3 well-filled cups of
dandelion flowers, picked
in a pesticide-free area
4 cups water
4 cups sugar

1 sachet pectin
2 tablespoons lemon juice
1 drop yellow food coloring
(optional, but without it the jam will
have a greenish color)

- Thoroughly wash the flowers and remove the sepals so they don't give the jam a bitter taste.
- Boil water in a medium-sized saucepan. Add half the flowers.
- Turn off the heat and leave to rest for 20 minutes.
- Using a fine sieve, remove the flowers and squeeze them well.
- Bring the water back to the boil and add the rest of the flowers.
- Cover, turn off the heat and let rest for 20 minutes.
- Remove the flowers, squeezing them as before.
- Measure 3 cups of the liquid and add sugar, lemon juice, pectin and the food coloring (if using). Put this back in the pan.
- Bring to the boil for one minute, stirring until the sugar dissolves. Remove the foam with a wooden spoon.
- Put the jam in sterilized jars, leaving a space the thickness of a finger at the neck of each jar. Keep in the fridge. This jam has the consistency of honey. If you prefer a thicker jam, add 1/2 cup of additional sugar (making a total of 4 and 1/2 cups).

Greater plantain and Ribwort plantain

(Plantago major, Plantago lanceolata)

This is a simple plant, short, without showy flowers or perfume. However, if you take the trouble to get to know it you will be rewarded with its many gifts. In either of its two forms, greater or ribwort, its leaves have long parallel veins that somewhat resemble the palm of a hand. They have great curative power: they can be used to help stop bleeding, mend wounds and regenerate the skin. So strong is this plant's healing power that it has been called "the bandage of the herbal world." It also serves to alleviate bites and scratches, make boils mature and help to expel splinters. A quick and easy treatment for minor skin lesions that hurt, burn or itch is to make a "saliva plaster": chew the leaves a little and apply the paste directly to the bite or affected area. Alternatively, you can wrap a leaf or a strip of one as a dressing around the wound.

Plantain is not just for external use. As an infusion it has a wide range of virtues: it is a general purifier of the system; it relieves colds, coughs, bronchitis, fever, hypertension, gastritis, cystitis, laryngitis, sinusitis, ulcers, hoarseness, diarrhea and rheumatism. Its astringent quality means that it can dry excessive secretions in the respiratory and digestive tract; but because it contains mucilage, it is much more kind to the organism than commercial astringents.

As if that isn't enough, it also helps lower cholesterol and triglyceride levels and stabilizes blood sugar. Some people use it to stop smoking, because purifying the body can help to decrease the cravings that cause recidivism.

It is also a nutritious vegetable: the leaves are rich in calcium and other minerals and vitamins, including vitamin K (giving it hemostatic properties). Young, tender leaves can be eaten in salads, but older ones should be cooked.

The seeds are harvested when they are ripe and can be used to add fiber and nutrients to your diet. For this, you can roast them or use them like chia seeds.

PLANTAIN CHIPS

24 large leaves of plantain, of any variety
2 tablespoons olive oil
1/4 teaspoon salt

1/2 teaspoon spices (garlic powder, nutritional yeast, pepper, cumin or whatever you prefer)

- Preheat the oven to 120°C/250°F.
- Wash the plantain leaves and dry them. In a large bowl mix the leaves with the oil.
- Arrange them on a baking sheet, in one layer. Sprinkle with salt and your chosen spices.
- Bake until they are crispy (not burnt). This may take 10 to 20 minutes, according to the size of the leaves. If in doubt it is preferable to take them out early, as they become crunchier as they dry out.
- Once cold, they can be stored in jars for several weeks. If they lose their crunchiness, bake them again for 3 to 5 minutes.

Plantain

NETTLE TONIC: A NUTRITIOUS INFUSION

- Pour a handful of dry nettles (as many as will fit in a fist— about 30 grams) in a one-liter jar with a lid.
- Fill with freshly boiled water, cover and leave to cool and macerate overnight.
- Strain and drink throughout the day, either hot or at room temperature. Note that this concoction does not taste especially good even when sweetened. It has a slight taste of earth (like chard or beetroot); if you look on this kindly you can consider it another of nettle's virtues!

Nettle

Nettle

(Urtica dioica)

The bad press suffered by the nettle is understandable, although wholly unjustified. It's true that when touched, the little hairs with which its leaves and stems are covered give off formic acid, causing brief but painful irritation to the skin. But nettles have so many good properties that it's worth putting on a pair of gloves and incorporating them into your diet.

Nettles have a very high content of iron, calcium and vitamin C. If you leave them to infuse overnight, a single cup will provide 250 milligrams of calcium (while an herb tea prepared in a few minutes only offers about five milligrams). Nettles also have useful amounts of protein and chlorophyll.

Nettles can also serve as food when cooked—they lose their sting within a few minutes. They make a good substitute for spinach and can be used in all kinds of preparations: stews, cakes, stuffed pastas, etc. Nettle soup is one of the most appetizing soups you'll ever taste, with a mild and delicious flavor . . . of fish! The emerald-green color of chlorophyll makes it a spectacle for the eyes too. You can add a pinch of sweet paprika and a touch of cream to set off the colors and complete the dish.

Above all, the nettle is an excellent medicinal plant with a bouquet of virtues: it is astringent, purifying, diuretic, anti-diabetic, anti-rheumatic, anti-asthmatic, expectorant, mildly laxative and hemostatic.

An excellent general tonic, this plant is a source of energy that is not as quickly used up as the more exciting burst of energy provided by sugar or coffee. In addition, it alkalinizes the blood and purifies the body, while also nourishing it. Thanks to its abundance of iron it is excellent for women during menstruation, or when they are pregnant or breastfeeding. High in iron and also in vitamin C, nettles are highly recommended for anemic states.

In other virtues, nettles strengthen bones, nails and hair; balance the hormonal, nervous and immune systems; normalize digestion; and relieve seasonal allergies. They also help coping with stress.

Nettle is a plant that should be taken daily to nourish the whole organism; to enjoy good energy with which to start the day, and to help achieve calm and restfulness to finish it.

Chickweed

(Stellaria media)

This little plant with small leaves and even smaller flowers grows in damp and shady places. Its scientific name comes from the star-shape of the flower, barely visible, but lovely if observed up close.

It is mainly eaten raw: its fresh and slightly salty taste goes well with any salad. In fact, it can form the basis of a salad by itself: just add tomatoes or any fresh vegetables that you have at hand. The whole plant can be used. Snipping it with scissors stimulates its growth, so it is advisable to cut it regularly.

It contains an important amount of vitamin C, and also vitamins A, B and D; and minerals such as iron, calcium and potassium. It also has various therapeutic actions: it is a tonic, diuretic, expectorant, antibacterial and mildly laxative. Its juice is a tonic for the eyes, and has traditionally been used to control excess weight because of its saponin content (saponins are chemical compounds found mostly in plants; studies have linked them to a reduction in body fat and cholesterol).

Applied externally, it relieves inflammation, itching and burns, and helps heal wounds.

Mugwort

(Artemisia vulgaris)

Mugwort is a native European plant that has become naturalized in the Americas and other parts of the world. It is considered a "lunar plant," with a feminine quality to it, perhaps because of its virtue of alleviating ailments of the female reproductive tract. It has a long tradition of magical uses. Legend has it that there was no witch (or herbalist, which is the same thing) who didn't have a patch of mugwort growing near her door.

Its Latin name honors the Greek goddess of the moon, who is evoked by the white underside of its leaves. In herbal tradition, one of its main virtues is to assist in dream recall and the capacity to promote lucid dreams (those in which you realize you are dreaming). For this, take as an infusion or place a cloth bag with its dried leaves under your pillow.

It is also excellent for cleaning and energizing environments. The herbalists of yesteryear used the plants after they had flowered for cleansing spaces, claiming that at this stage of its lifecycle the plant became more magical than medicinal.

As a medicine, mugwort is a digestive and expectorant, as well as being a great emmenagogue and antispasmodic, ideal for relieving menstrual cramps and regulating the menstrual cycle. It has a calming effect on the nerves and is good for fighting colds. To counteract its slightly bitter taste, it can be combined with lemon balm and other more palatable herbs.

Common Purslane
(Portulaca oleracea)

This succulent-like herb with reddish stems and tiny yellow flowers is almost as common as the dandelion, but it's not nearly as well known. Despite that, its tasty leaves have been used as food since prehistoric times and it is frequently mentioned in ancient treatises on Chinese medicine.

Fortunately, the best-kept secret of the plant world is beginning to be unveiled: common purslane has more omega-3 essential oils than some kinds of fish (which makes it an indispensable friend to vegetarians) and provides 17 vitamins and minerals, some powerful antioxidants (which combat different types of cancer) and four flavonoids that are only found in this plant. It is rich in fiber and one of the best sources of vitamin A of all green vegetables.

How do you eat it? In salads, combined with tomato or cucumber, olive and lemon (it is a classic of Greek cuisine). It can also be added to sautéed food (without cooking it too much because it becomes pasty due to its high mucilage content), and it can be preserved as a kind of pickle. Picked fresh, it lasts three or four days in the refrigerator, but the ideal is to cut sprigs of the plant as and when you need them, so as to get the full benefits of its nutritional potency.

Medicinally, the leaves and stems have a cardiotonic and expectorant effect; they are anti-inflammatory and diuretic. Its seeds reduce blood pressure, cholesterol, triglycerides and blood sugar.

A GREEN FIRST-AID KIT: THE INSTRUCTION BOOKLET

Well, we've harvested our plants! It is clear how much they can add to our daily diet. Now let's see the ways they can be prepared to heal the ailments that afflict us.

The active ingredients of the plants can be extracted in water, vinegar, oil, honey or alcohol (these are referred to as a "menstruum"). If you use alcohol as your menstruum, the result is a "tincture." Alcohol destroys the nutritional content of the plant, but it extracts and preserves the pharmacological actions, and it is the most powerful medicine you can prepare yourself at home (apart from making capsules, but this requires some equipment).

Let's start with the simplest procedure: making a medicinal infusion. This differs from making an herbal tea in the amount of the plant that is used and the length of time for which it is exposed to hot water. A tea bag is usually left in the water for about three minutes, while a medicinal infusion requires at least 15 or 20 minutes. Plants with a mild effect like nettle, oat straw or red clover need even longer: it is advisable to leave them for four hours, or even overnight, to make a more potent infusion.

The leaves and flowers are not themselves boiled: the water is brought to the boil, the heat is turned off and the plants are left to infuse in a covered container. The hard parts of plants (roots, seeds and barks), on the other hand, do need to be boiled for ten to fifteen minutes to release their goodness (this is called a "decoction"), or left to macerate overnight: the effect is the same. Whether you are making an infusion or a decoction, to boil the water it is advisable to use a glass, stainless steel, ceramic or iron container, not aluminum (aluminum can seep into the herbal preparation, making it toxic or robbing it of its properties).

Use approximately one tablespoon of the dried plant, or three tablespoons of fresh, per cup. If you want enough to drink the infusion throughout the day you will need 30 grams of plant material in a liter of water.

Medicinal infusions are best drunk at room temperature, unless the aim is to induce sweating, in which case they must be drunk hot.

For external use, you will need to prepare a lotion, compress, cream, ointment or a bath. Let's start with the oldest and simplest method, suitable for relieving the pain of a wound or itching caused by an injury, a rash or a sting: a saliva plaster. How is it done? Once you have identified the appropriate plant (plantain, mugwort, chickweed, yarrow or rose petals are some of the most common and most useful) you need to make a ball from it and chew it lightly so the juice is released and you can apply it to the affected area. It is not enough to crush it with your fingers; it is important that the plant comes into contact with your saliva.

You can also macerate or soak *yourself*, absorbing the medicinal property of the plants by immersing your body in an herbal bath. There are several ways to do this: make an infusion in a pot, strain and pour the liquid into the bathtub; hang a muslin bag containing the plants from the tap as you run the water; make bath salts, combining the chosen herbs with coarse salt; or throw the plants directly into the water. Some of the best plants to use for a bath are: oat straw (or even coarse oats, which you can buy easily in most food shops, and are nutritious, relaxing and emollient); sage, lavender or chamomile (sedatives); dandelion flowers (which purify the skin); mint (an energizing plant that helps heal wounds); and pine, rosemary or eucalyptus (decongestants).

For ritual as well as medicinal use, diverse native cultures of the past have inhaled the plants in the form of a smudge stick or pipe.

Keeping Plants

To dry leaves and roots, place them in paper bags (never plastic), in a semi-closed jar, or hang them outside, always in the shade. They can be stored when they are crisp. Important: a well-preserved plant has the color and aroma of the original plant. If you see a dried plant that looks like unidentifiable gray dust, it is likely that it has little or no vital energy left for healing.

The herbalist Susun Weed, author of the *Wise Woman* series of books, was participating in a panel discussion about menopause when a doctor, also on the panel, declared that no herb was safe to use unless its active ingredient was measured and standardized. This was Susun's answer:

> To me the active ingredient of a plant is the very part that cannot be measured: the energy, the life force, the chi, the fairy of the plant, not a "poisonous" constituent. To the healer/artist/herbalist, the active part of the plant is that part that can be used by the right brain to actively, chaotically, naturally, "jump the octave" and work a miracle. This active part is refined away in standardized products, for the real active part is the messy part, the changeable part, the subtle part, and the invisible part.

MAKING A TINCTURE

This is a simple procedure that uses alcohol to extract the maximum goodness possible from a plant (as opposed to tisanes or infusions, which can only extract properties that are soluble in water). A tincture can be made with fresh or dried plants. For the latter you use half the plant material as when using the fresh plant, because it will expand when you soak it in liquid.

Ingredients
- Fresh or dried plant material
- A glass bottle with a metal top
- Vodka or brandy, due to its high alcohol content. It doesn't have to be an expensive brand; cheaper varieties will work just as well. If you don't drink alcohol (or if you are going to give the tincture to a child), you can use apple cider vinegar instead, but you will lose some of the nutrients and components.
- Labels and a pen

Instructions
- Sterilize the bottle and fill it with your chosen plant. It is important to cut it into small bits (whichever part of the plant you are using, be it leaf, flower, stem or root) so that the maximum amount of the plant is in contact with the alcohol. Fill the bottle up to the neck with your chosen alcohol.
- Stir the mixture with a wooden spoon (or chopstick) so that there are no air bubbles left in it, and label it (writing the name of the plant and the date). Leave it to rest and macerate in a dark place for four to six weeks. It is advisable to keep it in a handy place, at least at the beginning, so that you remember to shake it. This is also a good time to connect with the energy of the plant and to imprint in the medicine your healing intention.
- After the maceration time, filter the mixture using a strainer wrapped in muslin or gauze. When you get to the end, squeeze the dregs of the liquid well so as not to waste a drop of the medicine. The remains of the plant can be put on the compost heap or added to a plant pot for nutrition.

- You can use a clean jar for the decanted liquid, or reuse the same jar, but it is important if you do this to change the label, this time adding the medicinal properties of the tincture so that you have it at hand ready for use when necessary.
- An herbal tincture needs to be diluted in two fingers of water for use. There are several ways of getting the dose you need. One is to drink the liquid two to three times a day, taking 20 to 30 drops of tincture at a time. Another, more practical, way is to: take one whole teaspoon of tincture (always diluted) per day, for chronic ailments, or half a teaspoon several times a day (or every hour, as needed) for acute pains or ailments.

Seasonal Harvests

Few experiences are as rewarding as "going out to harvest" and living in a city is no impediment. This is a brief sample of the variety of possible crops to be found in even the most urban of landscapes.

What you can harvest when will depend on your location—the climate, the soil and other conditions—but here are some ideas for plants that you may find. Note that the common names of plants vary greatly from place to place.

Spring

Lime tree leaves. With the first lime tree leaves of spring you can make "forest cookies."

FOREST COOKIES

50 grams all-purpose flour
125 grams sugar
125 grams butter
1 egg

1 tablespoon young lime leaves, without stems, cut into small pieces

- Mix the ingredients to make an even dough, roll it out flat and cut it in circles.
- Bake the cookies at medium heat until the edges are lightly browned.
- Sprinkle with icing sugar.

lime tree

Lime tree flowers. They can be used fresh to make an infusion (an elixir of the gods!), dried so you can make the same infusion in winter, or used to make lime tree honey. How? Easy! Separate the flowers from the stems and put them in a glass jar. Fill with honey up to the top, mix it with a wooden spoon and let it macerate for several weeks. It can be used from the start but it improves with time. There is no need to strain the flowers; they are delicious spread on toast.

Lime tree flowers and fruits. Mixing and processing green (unripe) lime tree fruits with dried flowers (from the same tree), in a proportion of 10–12 parts of fruit to one part of flowers, makes a carob-flavored paste. With the ripe fruits (they are ripe when they turn brown), you can make a coffee substitute.

Willow branches. Willow cuttings secrete auxin, a water-soluble hormone that stimulates root growth in other plants. Cut off some young twigs—the thickness of a pencil—from the tips of the branches where the buds are ready to bloom and put them in a glass jar. Pour boiling water on top and cover for 24 hours. Then strain it and you have your rooting hormone!

Various fruits of spring and early summer growing on trees you see on the sidewalk, which may include loquats and mulberries.

Summer

Aguaribay pink pepper. We use the drupes, or seeds on a stem, which look somewhat like a bunch of grapes. They can be collected from January and are useful to spice up all kinds of dishes. They have a sweet and peppery taste.

Blackberries: can be eaten raw, or cooked with apple, or used in jam.

Nettles, varieties of *Chenopodium* (lambsquarters, fat hen, etc) and other leafy vegetables. They are at their peak right at the beginning of summer and can be eaten raw or cooked.

Autumn

Acorns. Can be used to make flour, but the process to remove their bitterness is long and tiring. Better to use them to entertain children. Without much effort, they become goblins with hats, garlands or whatever comes to mind.

Araucaria pine nuts. They can be cooked in the oven or boiled. When they are soft (after about an hour), peel them and eat them with salt. Delicious!

Dandelion roots. An ideal activity to do as a family. Children enjoy digging up the roots and seeing them stored in glass jars (and roasted to make coffee). It makes them feel like they're visiting Hogwarts, the Harry Potter School of Wizardry. No wonder: they're the closest thing we have to preserved mandrakes. As if that weren't enough, although they don't contain caffeine, they do contain an interesting array of vitamins and minerals.

Hazelnuts. The edible ones are those that come wrapped in spiky shells. As tempting as it may be, it is best to wait a month after the autumn has begun—which is when the first ones will fall—to harvest them because the first ones are usually too small to make them worth the bother of peeling. In some places you may also find sweet chestnuts.

Rosehips. Full of vitamin C and are used to make tea or to flavor jams. In England they were used during the Second World War to prevent scurvy. The fleshy part is used and the seeds, which are something of an irritant, are discarded. Avoid plants that may have been sprayed with chemicals.

Hibiscus. Use to make magic hibiscus juice: take a red hibiscus flower, remove the corolla and pistil (the petals and seeds) and immerse it in freshly boiled water. It will infuse the water with a soft violet color. Then gather the children around it and quirt a bit of lemon in while you say an energetic "Abracadabra!" In an instant the juice will turn carmine-red! Once you have caught the children's attention, sweeten it, chill it and serve it as a (healthy, vitamin C-filled) juice. No child can resist it!

Winter

Pine needles. The needles of many types of conifers are edible—but not those of the Norfolk pine, which are poisonous. You can make a tea with them, or a tasty medicinal vinegar. Both are rich in vitamin C.

Eucalyptus seeds and leaves. These can be boiled in decoction to make vapors and inhalations to alleviate colds, or simply to purify environments.

Grains of paradise. The mature seeds of this tree are the raw material for an excellent pesticide. Macerate the seeds in water for two weeks, then dilute one part of the resulting liquid in five parts of water and spray on your flowerbeds; it keeps away ants and some of the other common "garden-eaters."

Chickweed, plantain, clovers and burdock roots are some other goodies available in cold weather.

We have reached the end of the vegetal route. For the next step of the journey we must put away our baskets and pick up binoculars instead, to step into a universe that is more volatile—but just as fascinating.

THE BROTHERHOOD OF BIRDS

Lord...
I have been, perhaps, a branch of a tree,
a bird's shadow,
the reflection of a river...
J. L. Ortiz

Birds live in our gardens, on our balconies, in our neighborhood trees. They offer city dwellers a wonderful opportunity to live alongside wild animals. And yet how many of us pass up this gift without opening it? We praise their inspired song; we envy their ability to fly; but mostly we lead our lives as if they didn't exist, or at least as if they were ornamental—beautiful but incidental—part of the scenery.

Other cultures are connected to the winged world in a different way. The San people, who live in the Kalahari Desert, explain it like this:

If one day I see a bird and I recognize it, a fine thread forms between us.
If I go out tomorrow and I recognize the same bird, the thread thickens

a little. Every time I see and I recognize the same bird the thread grows until it becomes a rope. We have ropes connecting us with all the aspects of creation, with the whole universe.

It may seem utopian to believe that those of us living in built-up areas could regain that level of connection with nature when we live so removed from the green nation and move at such a frenzied pace. Today, not only do we not tend to bond with the birds that surround us but we often suppose that the birds we come across are always different individuals that randomly cross our path. The opposite is true: because they are territorial animals, birds make their life in a home area with a radius of about 10 to 20 meters. Once they identify a place and recognize its hiding places, its sources of supply and shelter, they don't abandon it easily. Therefore, the birds we see every day are no more and no less than our neighbors. With a bit of patience and dedication we can learn to know them and even to distinguish one from another by some individual trait.

Why would we want to bond with birds? For our ancestors these animals were allies in their most important tasks: defending themselves against predators and detecting prey. Birds alerted them to the presence of both with their movements and sounds, and thus rendered humans an indispensable service. Today, we no longer need birds to survive, but if you can learn what professional tracker Jon Young calls "the deep language of the birds" (in his book *What the Robin Knows: How Birds Reveal the Secrets of the Natural World*), your world will acquire unsuspected wonders. What does he mean by "deep language"? He is talking about a species-to-species communication, full of information encoded in vocalizations and bodily gestures, that is practiced by the birds that surround us.

Young is an enthusiastic promoter of the idea of diving into nature in order to rediscover the native who lives in the heart of even the most entrenched city dweller. He has initiated a great many people in this art and in so doing has helped to give confidence and a sense of belonging to at-risk adolescents and members of other vulnerable groups, through trans-formative experiences in nature.

Young's first piece of advice for learning to re-establish the bond is simple: choose a "sit spot" close to home. It could be a bench in a square or a chair on your balcony, or in your garden. You should sit there every day for at least ten minutes, notebook in hand, to observe what happens. Young calls this "going out to listen to the news of the day."

At first you may not notice anything at all, but once you learn to silence your mind, you'll slowly start to read your environment like a musical score. To be able to observe birds' baseline behavior instead of always catching them mid-flight, you will have to learn to develop four simple skills:

Owl vision. This consists of broadening your field of vision: widening your gaze to include the periphery; trying to capture as much visual information as you can, without moving your head or your eyes. This reassures birds and invites them to carry on with their lives as if you were not there. If you are walking, a variation is to face the other way and look over your shoulder at the bird so it won't notice you observing it.

Deer hearing. To sharpen your hearing, try to distinguish between sounds near and far. This will allow you to gather information about what's going on with other birds that aren't in your immediate environment. You'll also be able to make connections between events happening in different parts of the neighborhood.

Fox walk. Put your heel down first and then, gradually, the ball of your foot. This step produces a silent and unobtrusive walk, and at the same time shelters you from stepping on something potentially harmful, as your foot will "feel" the ground before it descends completely.

These three techniques will provide you with a sort of cloak of invisibility so that you can watch nature in peace. More importantly, they will generate a state of relaxation similar to that of any other contemplative practice (extra points if you discover this state before the last chapter, "The Lighthouse"!). Young says that a common mistake made by people when they start birdwatching is trying to be "stealthy." Stealth alerts a bird to your presence because it is the attitude of a predator; what you seek is not stealth, but a state of inner peace and silence.

In any expedition to observe nature it helps to visualize two circles: one representing the circle of your perception, and the other the disruption caused by your presence. The idea is to enlarge the first circle as much as possible, and shrink the second in order to achieve the perfect sweet spot that enables you to watch wildlife unobtrusively.

In his book, Young talks about the experience of a young man from a slum area of New York who took his course as part of a social program. At the end of the first ten-minute observation period, the boy had not written down a single event. "Nothing happened," he said, laconic and bored. On the second day, he wrote in his notebook that "a bird flew past me to my right." After a week, he was already able to distinguish the thrush from the great kiskadee and to record that the one had stolen food from the other a few meters from his bench, while parrots cackled excitedly in the branches of a eucalyptus. This small transformation bears witness to the fact that when we pay attention, the world expands; it becomes populated with beings, teeming with life. By applying these practices, Young says, "Birds become barometers for our awareness of the inner and outer landscape."

They also produce another unexpected result: the child within you is suddenly revived, as if invited to play after years of confinement. Who doesn't dream of being an explorer and going out to discover the secrets of the universe; more so when those secrets fly past in front of our noses?

Let us see what we can learn from the winged kingdom, without the need for books or binoculars, through the sheer force of listening and curiosity.

Birds and Their Language

There are five types of sounds that we can learn to recognize:

Song. This is by far the most studied—and enjoyed—of all bird sound. It differs from the call in duration and complexity. Each bird has a basic "repertoire" of songs and calls, but this includes many variations according to the time of day, as we shall see.

Companion call. This is the sound birds use to communicate with each other and to announce to their peers their location or where to find tasty snacks. It is very recognizable in the great kiskadee: a high-pitched whistle that alerts the whole neighborhood (as well as its addressee). Subtlety is not one of the attributes of this species.

Juvenile begging. This is a chick's hunger cry. It is emitted with an open beak, in the nest or when running behind a parent as the chick takes its first steps. You hear it mainly in spring, in the breeding season, and it is not necessary to train your ear much to recognize it. It is so clear that it awakens maternal instincts even in non-feathered animals.

Aggression. This is emitted especially by males, in reaction to territorial threats. Often it accompanies a ritual display that seeks to dissuade an intruder or to mark territory rather than develop into a physical conflict. Birds, both male and female, are renowned for the displays they make to protect their nests, sometimes to warn off predators several times bigger than themselves.

Cry of alarm. There are different cries for different occasions. Some species have a specific alarm for terrestrial dangers and another for aerial threats. The click that thrushes make when a human intruder gets too close to a nest also belongs in this category.

In order to be able to recognize these different sounds it is necessary to first learn to discern the "baseline" of each species: its habitual behavior when all is calm and life is normal. Once you have learned to recognize this, it is easier to detect when something is happening that deserves your attention.

A good opportunity to observe that baseline is when birds are eating. You can take advantage of that moment to study their body language and sounds, so that you can contrast them with other behaviors when they appear.

The mystery of birdsong

Birdsong is a fascinating and mysterious form of behavior. We may ask: why do they sing? After all, singing is an activity that requires a lot of energy and can attract the attention of predators. There are two main reasons on which ornithologists agree: to defend territory and to attract potential mates. For the male, singing with vigor and dexterity is a way of showing off his attributes and getting females to listen to him.

But there is another way of looking at this, proposed by professor of music and philosophy David Rothenberg. In his book *Why Birds Sing*, Rothenberg accepts the reasons given by science, but allows himself to speculate about a third option. He says:

Why do birds sing? For the same reasons we sing—because we can. Because we love to inhabit the pure realm of sound. Because we must sing—it's the way we have been designed to tap into the pure shapes of sound. We celebrate this ability in our greatest tasks, defining ourselves, defending our places, calling out to the ones we love. But form remains far more than function.

When he speaks of "form," Rothenberg is referring to the almost implausible elaboration and ornamentation of some songs. It is difficult to imagine why the lyrebird of Australia needs to perfectly imitate dozens of sounds (of other birds, of other things in nature and also of elements of civilization such as flutes, cameras, car alarms and chainsaws) in order to be considered a fit mate by one of the exquisite females.

It is not only song that seems to overcome utilitarian arguments: there is also the sense of aesthetics of the bowerbird of Australia and New Guinea, which color their nests with objects they find on the forest floor; and the choreographic talent of birds of paradise, found in the same corner of the world, which perform dance steps that could have inspired Michael Jackson's moonwalk.

Could it be that some birds just enjoy singing, dancing, flying and displaying their beauty and their gifts? Let's make room for that possibility in the infinite mystery of the world. Nevertheless, it must be said that courtship songs are the most striking. In almost all species it is the males that sing (except in the tropics, where both members of the pair sing in duet, and among Argentinian ovenbirds). The most spectacular displays occur in spring: first for sexual conquest and then to mark territory.

Songbirds are blessed with a syrinx (the avian version of the larynx), an organ located where the trachea divides into the bronchial tubes. Each side of the syrinx produces independent sounds, allowing a bird to emit two different tones at the same time. Some birds can even sing ascending and descending notes simultaneously. One species, the northern cardinal (Cardinalis cardinalis), can sing more notes than there are on a piano in a tenth of a second.

Although each species has a "base song," when a colony is isolated from the rest by some geographical accident its members may end up developing their own "dialect," which they then pass on to their offspring. That is why birds of the same species can intone different melodies. Can we sensitize our hearing enough to hear these variations?

On YouTube there are many recordings of songs and sounds of a variety of bird species. Listening to them is a way of training your ear to recognize those which live in your vicinity. You have probably heard them thousands of times, but without relating the bird to the song.

Here are some birds with well-defined songs that you might listen out for depending where you are in the world: rufous-collared sparrow, sparrow, thrush, great kiskadee, song thrush, blackbird, skylark.

Legendary songs

Birds have inspired countless myths and legends, many of which try to explain the diversity of habits, songs and customs of the different species. An example of this is a legend from north-eastern Argentina that explains why grayish baywings seem to be rehearsing when they sing as a flock and why the shiny cowbird usurps other birds' nests.

It is said that everything goes back to the day on which God taught the birds to make their nests and the night when the *vizcacha* [a mountain rodent] organized a great party for all the animals. Only the shiny cowbirds and the baywings accepted the invitation. The first because they were seduced immediately when they heard the words "feast." The second, because they liked to sing a lot.

The party was held late at night, when the rest of the birds were sleeping soundly, preparing themselves for the exhausting day ahead in which God was going to teach them how to build their respective nests. The baywings chose a great repertoire to liven up the party but they didn't get to perform. Their rehearsal lasted longer than it should have because they wasted a lot of time tuning their voices. Before the party could begin, God awoke all the birds at dawn for the task at hand.

The obedient baywings had to leave the party and go to work without having managed to sing a single song. Their cousins, the shiny cowbirds, ignored the order and remained at the party, never learning to build their nests. This explains why baywings only know how to rehearse. They only sing in groups and their singing sounds as if they are eternally tuning their instruments.*

Invite children to write legends that "explain" some of the habits and shapes of different birds: why ovenbirds make such peculiar nests; how hummingbirds choose the flowers they sip from; why woodpeckers drill holes into trees; why ravens leave people presents. These are just a few ideas to get you started!

* www.avesdelnea.blogspot.com

A Day in the Life of a Bird

Any of us could tell stories (nice or not) about our neighbors. And in the same way, we can tell stories about the birds that live near us. Just as we have established that they are not random individuals but always the same thrushes, robins and mockingbirds, we can also say that their movements are not casual and that their behavior is not aimless.

Birds are vulnerable animals and cannot afford to make large displays using unnecessary energy, so almost all their movements have a specific purpose. Therefore, their routines tend to follow recognizable patterns that we might observe.

What's a day like in the life of a bird? More or less like this:

- Before dawn, the great majority intone the "dawn chorus." It is the most elaborate song of the day, almost as if they were welcoming the sun. Some ornithologists speculate that it is a way to mark territory before the hustle and bustle of the day begins. Those of us with a more romantic inclination suspect other motives.
- Mid-morning is the time to feed. Birds that eat worms and crawling and ground insects will feed on the ground; others will perch on branches to peck at seeds, fruits and other insects. What you will hear at this point is a "harmonic cacophony" of layered voices, full of purpose and engagement.
- In the early afternoon, when the sun is high, birds tend to keep quiet and rest. At this time you will only hear crickets, cicadas and the cooing of pigeons.
- With the sunset, the bustle of activity returns. The chorus at dusk is somewhat less elaborate than that of the dawn, but—in some seasons—just as energetic and ear-catching.
- After sunset, each bird looks for a safe place to sleep. Birds don't sleep in nests—which are purely and exclusively for breeding and sheltering their offspring—but on tree branches and fences; or in shrubs, tree cavities, and other places hidden from predators and dangers. Some species sing songs in one area and then retreat to another, in order to mislead their predators. On the other hand, nocturnal species such as owls and birds of prey become active and go hunting when the sun goes down.

- How do they sleep without falling off their branches? As a gift of evolution, birds have developed a system for this. When a bird supports the weight of its body on its claws it activates a mechanism that locks the claws around the branch, as firm as a carpenter's vice. Waterfowl have an equally clever technique: they sleep as a flock on the water, keeping each other warm, and the birds on the outside of the group remain in a state of semi-sleep (with a part of their brain active and vigilant). If a predator approaches, they feel the vibration of the waves through the water and they alert the others.

This basic information should be enough to set you off researching more about bird behavior. Here are some practical suggestions:

BIRD ACTIVITIES

Field research

Observe and study the routine of the thrushes, swallows and sparrows that visit your balcony or live in your city block or garden:

- In which tree or corner do they sleep at night?
- Where do you first hear them in the morning?
- Where do they build their nests?
- What are their nests like?
- How many litters of offspring do they have?
- Which member of the couple (male or female) hatches them?
- How much time do they spend with their chicks?
- What do they feed them?
- Which predators cause them alarm? How far do they fly away when a cat, a dog or a person passes by? How long does it take them to come back? This is a measure of the concern that each of these predators produces.
- Can you recognize a vocalized sound of complaint or of alarm in such situations?
- How do they react when a train or plane passes by? Hint: when such loud sounds are heard, some predatory birds (such as hawks) take advantage of it to fly from one place to another without being detected. The same sound produces an urge to flee, often in flocks, in birds that are preyed upon.

Mapping the territory

This is a good activity to do with children.

The participants choose a space to map: it can be a city block or larger area. Different zones or territories are designated within that space and assigned to the participants. Each person stakes out his territory and devotes ten minutes to observing the behavior and language of the birds within it. At the end of that time, everyone assembles to share their observations and mark them on a simple diagram or map. The resulting map will show the movements of birds from one place to another and the avian "events" of that morning or afternoon, within the designated area.

Trush

Create a habitat for wildlife in the garden

You can help birds, insects and other animals by creating a garden that shelters and feeds them.

Here are some possibilities: provide fresh water in the form of a drinking trough or pond; offer food in a feeding trough (one option: hanging pinecones smeared with peanut butter and covered in a variety of seeds) or simply plant native flowers from which the birds and the bees can sip.

It is also advisable to avoid spraying the garden with pesticides; to mark windows with stickers so that the birds don't collide with them and hurt themselves; and to leave an overgrown area to provide shelter and nesting places.

In spring you can supply baskets filled with mosses and grasses, or even pieces of wool (not more than two centimeters long), for them to line the inside of their nests with. In the few weeks following you can go around the neighborhood and see if you can find nests "adorned" with your offerings. Whether you find them or not, going out looking for nests is in itself a beautiful experience.

Great kiskadee

SKY HIGH: THE SUBTLE CHARM OF CLOUDS

"What is a sunset without clouds? A circle that crosses a straight line," says Gavin Pretor-Pinney, founder of the Cloud Appreciation Society, creator of an original form of activism and of a manifesto that begins: "We believe that clouds are unjustly maligned and that life would be immeasurably poorer without them."

Clouds? Could they really be a motive for activism? At first glance it might seem at least curious that someone would want to devote his life to convincing his fellow Earthlings to look up and marvel at the spectacle of altocumulus, altostratus and cumulonimbus. But we only have to go back to childhood to understand. Who among us didn't spend long moments lying on the grass identifying rabbits, mountains and unicorns in the fanciful forms drawn across the sky? Who was not surprised to see how those images transformed themselves from one moment to the next before our eyes? Or perhaps a better question would be: when did clouds stop captivating us? When did we stop raising our eyes to the sky?

Clouds have always been a source of inspiration and wonder. Not for nothing have they featured in works of art across the centuries. Starting in the Renaissance, they even came to be used as metaphors for the divine. But why should we as adults learn to live again with our heads in the clouds? Purely in terms of common sense, obvious answers include: because identifying the shapes and types of clouds allows us to predict the chance of rain and to know whether we can expect a hailstorm, or a light but incessant drizzle that will cause moss to grow in unexpected places. This would indeed be good reason to look up at clouds; but it barely scrapes the surface of their potential.

We don't want to look at clouds to divine the weather forecast; we want to look at them so that we can dream again and remember that magic and beauty surrounds us at every step. We want to find in them a route back into wonder. "It is the time you have wasted for your rose that makes your rose so important," says Antoine de Saint-Exupéry's Little Prince. Let's waste time learning to love the world, every day, a little bit more and better. Let's waste time on what's truly important!

Allow me to act as an informal tourist guide to the main cloud families. It will not be an exhaustive tour, but with luck it will tempt you to continue exploring.

Like plants and animals, clouds are classified by the Linnaean system; in this case, according to their altitude and appearance. There are ten groups, known as "genres." Then there are a variety of "species" within each genre, and within each species there are also "varieties." As if that wasn't enough, there are also some other qualities that are sometimes added to the label. And all of it in Latin. If you are going to dedicate an afternoon to looking at clouds, it is well worth learning their taxonomy.

First things first: what is a cloud?

A cloud is a condensation of water vapor that is formed by the cooling of air. Condensation takes the form of droplets or particles of visible ice, so small that they are held aloft by light, vertical currents. Thermal currents also determine the formation of clouds: clouds created in still air take the form of layers, or strata, while those that form between winds develop upwards, in the shape of towers.

The simplest and most comprehensive classification is that which divides the clouds according to appearance between high, medium and low. Let's start with those closest to us!

Low Clouds

Cumulus

These are those cottony clouds, with clear and defined edges, that we all draw in our portraits of the sky when we are children. *Cumulus* means "mound" or "heap" and alludes to the "piled up" or "lumpy" form typical of this genre. They usually appear individually, although sometimes they group together and form patterns (such as the beautiful *cumulus radiatus*, which are the kind you see lined up in rows like streets). Seen against the sun they look bright white, but they can appear grey or dark if they have the sun behind them.

Let's look at some features and curiosities of this genre.

How much does an average cumulus weigh? The equivalent of 80 elephants. This is not a completely random association, explains Pretor-Pinney, because, according to ancient Hindu and Buddhist beliefs, cumulus are the spiritual cousins of elephants. For millennia Hindus have worshipped this animal and asked it to bring rain in the torrid summers of their part of the world. *Megha* ("cloud" in Hindi) is how elephants are addressed in these propitiatory prayers. Ancient creation myths say that in the beginning, elephants were white and had wings; they could change shape at will and they brought rain. Although they have clearly lost this ability, they are still considered to be related to clouds, particularly albino elephants.

How long does an average cumulus last? Ten minutes. The exception is *cumulonimbus*, a sort of reloaded cumulus, which can last for several hours. If several "cells" of clouds come together and form an agglomeration, it can persist even longer.

Where do they appear? All over the world, except in Antarctica, where the earth is too cold for the formation of thermal currents.

Cumulus are subdivided according to their size:

Cumulus humilis. Wider than they are tall, with a flat base and a cauliflower-shaped top. They tend to scatter in the sky in a random way. They are the classic "fair-weather" clouds: diaphanous, spongy and perfectly harmless. Pretor-Pinney says: "Don't be brainwashed by the sun fascists—fair-weather cumulus have a starring role in the perfect summer's day." If they stay small, there's no chance of rain. But if a *cumulus humilis* grows and has become a *cumulus congestus* by noon, there is a good chance that you will have to get out your umbrella in the afternoon. The mnemonic rule is: "In the morning mountain; in the afternoon fountain."

Cumulus mediocris. As tall as they are wide. They can have protuberances in various forms at the top.

Cumulus congestus. Taller than they are wide. They cause brief showers, but they can continue to grow and become the Tyrannosaurus rex of the heavens: the justly feared *cumulonimbus*.

Cumulonimbus

"Tyrannosaurus" is not actually a nickname that does this type of cloud justice. For its beauty and its bearing, we could instead call the *cumulonimbus* "the empress of the clouds." *Cumulonimbus* clouds can measure up to 18,000m high (higher than Mount Everest!). Their characteristic shape is that of a mushroom with a flattened top, or an anvil. The best way to recognize a cumulonimbus is by what it produces: it unleashes a fury of thunder, lightning, wind and sometimes hail.

How do you distinguish a *cumulus congestus* from a *cumulonimbus*? If the upper part of the cloud still has precise edges (cauliflower-shaped) it is a *congestus*. If it flattens and becomes diffuse, beware: it is a *cumulonimbus*.

High up inside these clouds there may be large ice crystals. If anyone could attest to this fact, it was Lieutenant Colonel William Rankin, a U.S. Air Force pilot, veteran of the Second World War, who was the first and (so far) only person to fall through the belly of a *cumulonimbus* and survive.

It sounds like science fiction but, incredibly, it's true. On 26 July 1959 Rankin was flying his F-8 Crusader over the top of a storm cloud when suddenly the engines failed and the fire warning light came on. He tried to control the plane with the emergency lever, but he pulled it and it came away in his hands. He had no choice but to eject from the aircraft at an altitude of 14,000m, without a pressure suit and knowing that outside he would meet temperatures of 50 degrees below zero—along with the prospect of seeing an electric thunderstorm up front and center.

It was 6 p.m. sharp when he shot himself out of the plane. He suffered immediate frostbite, especially in one hand, from which the glove blew off as he left the cockpit. Decompression caused him to bleed from his eyes, nose and mouth, and his stomach to swell painfully to the size of a nine-month pregnancy. He tried to put off triggering his parachute until he had descended low enough to use it, but it yanked itself open at 3,000m, and an icy rush of air pushed him helplessly towards the heart of the storm. Rain and hailstones battered Rankin from all sides and there was so much water around him that he had to hold his breath in order not to drown. The hurricane winds spun him round like a puppet, making him vomit from the dizziness. He could only see a meter around him, and more than hearing the thunder, he reported, he felt its impact all over his body.

But what he would remember most, as he narrates in his book *The Man Who Rode the Thunder*, were the bolts of lightning. He describes them as ropes of blue fire half a meter wide that exploded around him like fireworks. At one point he looked up just as a lightning bolt illuminated his parachute: he saw a floodlit vault in the middle of the blackness and thought that he had finally died.

But he hadn't. He was alive and about to emerge from the belly of the beast. Suddenly the waters calmed down, the temperature climbed several degrees and he began to feel his extremities again. As he looked up at the cloud tower above him he realized that he was descending gently toward the Earth beneath his parachute.

But nothing was going to be easy that day. A few meters before touching the ground a gust of wind picked him up and crashed him into the top of a tree. Fortunately, his helmet saved him from losing consciousness. He managed to get down from the tree and looked at his watch: it was 6:40. A descent of that distance would normally take ten minutes. Rankin had spent 40 minutes traveling through the inside of the *cumulonimbus*, and he had lived to tell the tale.

Rankin lived for a further five decades, having gone through an adventure that few people will ever experience. Thank God.

Stratus

These are low clouds that extend like ceilings over fields and cities. They produce a soft and constant drizzle and give a sensation of pressure and claustrophobia, since they hide the perspective and the height of the sky from view.

Pretor-Pinney confesses that it frustrates him not to be able to love this particular cloud formation: "It's like that kind of friend who stays too long and doesn't know when to leave." However, these are the clouds that come closest to the Earth and to which we owe fog and mist. In addition, when they finally clear, they remind us how wonderful the sun is!

In autumn and winter, stratus clouds can remain in the sky for the whole day; but in spring and early summer you usually see them only in the early hours of the morning and then they disperse for the rest of the day. In this, they are a harbinger of good weather.

Their varieties are: opaque (when they hide the sun and the moon); translucent (when they are thin and you can see the sky through them); and *undulatus* (when they have a curly shape).

Stratocumulus

These clouds form low, cottony-shaped layers. In their most spectacular version they are called *lenticularis,* which are shaped like a UFO and often form around mountain peaks. Some people think that many supposed images of UFOs are actually *stratocumulus lenticularis* in all their glory.

Medium-Altitude Clouds

Altocumulus

The name may suggest that these are high clouds but in fact they are only mid-height. They usually take the form of "buns" scattered across the sky. They come in two varieties—*stratiformis undulatus* and *lenticularis*—that differ in altitude. They usually announce rain or even a storm.

Altostratus

These are thin layers of clouds with some dense areas, but with almost no texture. They are known as "the boring clouds" and they produce a fine and persistent "London-style" rain, along with a drop in temperature. In general they allow a glimpse of the sun. At sunset, even an altostratus can make an impressive spectacle.

The varieties of altostratus include *radiatus, opacus, translucidus, undulatus* and *duplicatus* (when the form is duplicated).

Nimbostratus

These are the classic rainy-day clouds (*nimbus* means rain): thick gray or dark layers that release water as a constant and steady shower.

Unlike *cumulonimbus* they never catch you unawares, without an umbrella, because they make it clear what you can expect from the outset.

If *cumulonimbus* delivers a furious torrent of short duration, nimbus clouds wears you down with exhaustion. While the former looms above in the shape of a tower, the nimbus appears as a kind of endless carpet.

High Clouds

Cirrus

These are white, shiny and transparent clouds with a fine striated, silky appearance. They are composed of ice crystals that half-freeze while falling through the sky, and give the impression that an ambitious painter has used the firmament as a canvas. Earth shares these clouds with other planets; notably Mars, Jupiter, Saturn and Uranus.

Their varieties include: *fibratus* (meaning fibrous), *uncinus* (reminiscent of waves or hair—for which they are sometimes called mares' tails) and the crazy-looking *vertebratus* (like a fish skeleton stretched across the sky).

When *cirrus* fill the sky, you can bet that in less than 24 hours there will be a sharp drop in temperature.

Cirrocumulus. These clouds form an almost continuous layer, with fine wrinkles and rounded shapes. They are completely white, without a shadow.

Cirrocumulus frequently appear next to cirrus and usually indicate a change in the state of the weather in the following 12 hours—they often precede a storm.

Cirrostratus. This type have the appearance of a veil across the sky, with some occasional long and wide striation. The edges have defined and regular limits. They usually produce a halo in the sky around the sun or moon. *Cirrostratus* usually follow cirrus and herald the arrival of bad weather as storms or warm fronts.

Unusual Clouds

Morning glory

These are unusual formations that sometimes occur on the north Australian coast off Burketown, around September and November. They are roll-shaped clouds that can be up to 1,000 kilometers long (making them one of the largest formations in the world) and move at a speed of 60 kph, close to sea level. Sometimes they generate formations of up to eight "rolls" aligned in parallel. Hang-gliding professionals travel to Burketown in those months of the year in the hope of flying over the clouds.

"New" Clouds

Every so often someone spots a type of cloud that doesn't fit into the standard classification system. This is the case with the 11 new formations that were admitted to the *International Cloud Atlas* (the hall of fame of clouds) in 2017. The incorporation of cameras into mobile phones has led to new generations of "itinerant scientists" who record cloud sightings, extending the available database to include new discoveries.

Is it important to name new clouds? Pretor-Pinney says: "This interest in naming the clouds helps us to connect with the atmosphere and the world; while understanding it more, we know it more and we care more. At the same time, it counteracts the pressures of the digital world, because when we look at the sky we are distracted from the pressures of the Earth."

If they had known this, perhaps our mothers wouldn't have scolded us so much for having our heads in the clouds. This early indication of our true vocation has no doubt equipped us to become first-class "cloud-spotters." Pretor-Pinney would be proud of us all.

A Naturalist's Journal

In some ways the journals of the 18th-century naturalists, with their detailed line drawings of the flora and fauna of their own countries or the territories they visited, are the forerunners of modern biology. But you don't need to be a scientist to use the same method of reconnection, which is as simple as it is effective. All you need to do is observe the nature that surrounds you and the events of each season, and record what you see in a notebook.

You can accompany your observations with photos or drawings. The important thing is to write down everything that catches your attention: each plant, cloud or animal, its interactions with its surroundings and the emotions it arouses in you. In so doing you will broaden your knowledge by learning to identify what you see in the natural world in the same empirical way used by the first scientists; but you will also strengthen your connection to nature by improving the quality of your attention. It is essential to note the date of each entry. Then you will know if the chickweed is flowering early this season; if the *cirrus fibratus* stamped on the sky at dawn anticipates rain or good weather; and if the pair of sparrows that live on your block like to move to a different tree each time they build a new nest. To study nature is to get to know it, and to love it more with each passing day.

Let us go back to swinging back and forth between heaven and Earth, like the children we once were. Back to lying on the grass; to letting the wind play in our hair; to wearing play clothes made of pollen and dew. It really is never too late to come home.

THE GARDEN
Awaken Your Senses

i thank You God for most this amazing
day: for the leaping greenly spirits of trees
and a blue true dream of sky; and for everything
which is natural which is infinite which is yes

. . .

(now the ears of my ears awake and
now the eyes of my eyes are open)
e e cummings

The thick foliage gradually diminishes and as you move forward the sun reappears between the leaves. The trees here are arranged in rows and each row offers a different fruit. At knee height, meanwhile, tomatoes rub shoulders with basil, rosemary and marigolds. Over there, potatoes and carrots pierce the earth, growing upside down. The aromas are intoxicating; the colors vibrate with their contrasts; the air carries the scent of grass and the warm temperature invites you to linger here. You are in a garden: a treat for the eyes, the ears, the skin . . . and for the soul.

Your senses are gateways from the world to your own personal ecosystems. It is largely thanks to them—sight, smell, taste, touch, and at least a dozen other faculties that we barely know about—that we are the beings we are: sentient, restless, excitable; and capable of being hurt or infinitely moved.

Emotions and thoughts are nourished by them, more than we know. When we move away from their influence—when we stop looking, listening, tasting, and surrender to worries—the heart aches.

However, for most of us life allows no time to stop to notice and receive ephemeral impressions; always in a hurry to achieve some more urgent goal, we tend to overlook the input of the senses. It is a persistent delusion to be always on the way to somewhere better.

Even if we wanted to, we probably wouldn't be capable of consciously registering 100 percent of the information that the senses bring to us. Jorge Luis Borges' short story "Funes the Memorious," about a character unable to filter and forget his memories, suggests that a life in which every impression makes its mark would become unlivable. But it is possible to resist the sensory numbing that modern living affords us.

We are products of a culture that values intellect, action, consumption, immediate rewards and, increasingly, virtual reality. It is easy to spend a whole day lounging in an armchair, or seated before a desk, your body immobile and your gaze fixed on a screen, and yet still feel as if you have *got a lot done* or *visited a lot of places*. These digital excursions are not at all similar to journeys of the imagination, in which there is experience, creativity, discovery; they are more like passively enjoying a ride in an amusement park.

You watch a zebra running with the herd in a high-definition documentary and you believe you are *sharing the experience* with the animals. But what is an experience worth when it lacks depth, perspective, smell, texture and temperature? This is not to deny the many advantages of technology but to balance things up a little in favor of our ancient and basic *animal nature.*

For our ancestors, the senses were tools of survival. Their noses brought them the smell of food and danger; their ears warned them of predators and avalanches; their taste buds distinguished between a tasty mouthful and a potentially lethal one. Today almost all information that reaches us is mediated by the intellect, while our bodies remain lethargic, waiting for some stimulus to shake them out of drowsiness.

In reality, our senses supply us with as much information today as before, but we learn less because we don't pay them the same amount of attention. Or, perhaps, we don't treat them with the same *quality* of attention.

In her autobiographical book, *Long Life: Essays and Other Writings,* the poet Mary Oliver explains how she learned the difference between two kinds of attention from her partner, photographer Molly Malone:

> It has frequently been remarked, about my own writings, that I emphasize the notion of attention. This began simply enough: to see that the way the flicker flies is greatly different from the way the swallow plays in the golden air of summer. It was my pleasure to notice such things, it was a good first step. But later, watching M. when she was taking photographs, and watching her in the darkroom, and no less watching the intensity and openness with which she dealt with friends, and strangers too, taught me what real attention is about. Attention without feeling, I began to learn, is only a report. An openness—an empathy—was necessary if the attention was to matter.

The Jungian psychologist James Hillman warned of the same thing with the words, "We have lost the heart's response to what the senses bring to us."

Let us see, then, how we can use our whole being to *pay attention* to life and to allow the senses to once again illuminate and inform our hearts.

How many senses do we have? There is no absolute agreement on the answer to this question. In addition to the five usual suspects—hearing, taste, touch, smell and sight—it is known that we have the faculties of thermoreception (ability to perceive temperature); proprioception (awareness of one's movements); nociception (sense of pain); pruriception (sensation of itching); equilibrioception (sense of balance); and other subtler perceptions such as the ability to detect the oxygen concentration, salt or carbon dioxide levels in our blood. Some people even argue that we should acknowledge chronoception (ability to perceive the passage of time).

Although it would be fascinating to explore these unknown sensory worlds, just to bring your full attention to the five generally recognized senses will substantially enrich your life.

SMELL

I enter the kitchen, ready to take advantage of the early-morning calm to write. My thoughts still swim in the waters of sleep and I feel far away in my own world. Still dozing, I prepare coffee. When it's ready I sit down and lift the cup to my mouth. The sensation triggered by that aroma is curious: flashes of wakefulness wrapped in warmth. *Hygge*, I think.

When I was a girl, I was crazy about the aroma of coffee. I would smell it percolating in the kitchen and my nose would follow its perfume, like the children who trailed behind the Pied Piper. I tried drinking it several times, but spat it out every time in disappointment. How could the bitterness of that taste be connected to the promise of that scent? Years later, at university, I overcame my resistance and used coffee as an ally in pre-examination vigils. At the same time, my study group began to meet at the home of Silvina, a friend who was of Sephardic ancestry. Silvina's mother visited us at regular intervals with trays of Turkish coffee and several kinds of sweet treats, just as her ancestors would have done. The tray was round, golden, made of embossed metal. I think the spell of that tray marked the beginning of my love affair with the brew. "The smell of coffee cooking was a reason for growing up," as the African American chef Edna Lewis said. I had definitely grown up.

Of the five main senses, smell is the most directly connected to the emotions. There are physiological reasons: the olfactory bulb, lodged in the nose, is connected to two areas of the brain associated with memory and emotion, the amygdala and the hippocampus. Thus the scent of jasmine is more likely to evoke the memory of your grandmother's balcony than seeing a photo of the same flower.

Human beings can recognize more than 10,000 smells and we have 1,000 olfactory receptors that constantly regenerate throughout our lives. Smell is also one of the few senses that is always active, whether you want it to be or not: every time you breathe—more than 23,000 times a day—you are detecting smells. In the seconds it takes you to inhale, a small army of molecules floats into your system. At the same time, other molecules emanate *from* you: we live immersed in a sea of smells.

The olfactory world does not, of course, only consist of pleasing aromas; it also includes less pleasant smells. Between the *perfume* of flowers and the *stink* of garbage there is a sensory world of difference. At least for adults; babies are decidedly less picky.

Why?

Maybe there's something instinctive about our rejection of certain smells. Plato was one of the first to associate the sense of smell with our animal condition, assigning it a low place among human experiences. Similarly, "Along with lechery, desire and impulse, smell bears the stamp of the animal," wrote an anonymous author at some point in history. Why associate smell with our instinctive nature? On the one hand, animals are highly dependent on smell to eat, mate and recognize territory. On the other hand, the physiological links between the centers of smell and language in the brain are so poor that it is hard for us to put words to what we smell. The sense of smell is thus distanced from those qualities that we consider quintessentially human.

In her marvelous poetic-scientific exploration, *A Natural History of the Senses,* the naturalist Diane Ackerman points out some curious paradoxes of smell:

> We don't require smell to mark territories, establish hierarchies, recognize individuals or, especially, know when a female is in heat. And yet one look at the obsessive use of perfume and its psychological effect on us makes it clear that smell is an old warhorse of evolution we groom and feed and just can't let go of. We don't need it to survive, but we crave it beyond all reason, maybe, in part, due to a nostalgia for a time when we were creatural, a deeply connected part of Nature.

Smell is part of taste. When you inhale deeply, in the middle of enjoying something richly tasty to eat, you send the air to the olfactory receptors in your nose so that you can "smell it better." Without smell there is no taste: were you to taste the most exquisite of wines with your sense of smell switched off, it would taste like water.

We have highly personal olfactory predilections: we like the aroma of people we love and sometimes we are even capable of recognizing them with our eyes shut. A baby smells its mother as she enters the room, long before it sees her. In many languages the word for "kissing" is the same as the word for "smell," and there is speculation that the kiss began as an extension of the act of smelling each other's faces—which have a high concentration of olfactory receptors. The ritual rubbing of noses among the Inuit (improperly known as Eskimos) is an illustration of this.

The deaf and blind writer and activist Helen Keller wrote how smell served as a portal to intimacy with the world:

> Masculine exhalations are, as a rule, stronger, more vivid, more widely differentiated than those of women. In the odor of young men there is something elemental, as of fire, storm, and salt sea. It pulsates with buoyancy and desire. It suggests all the things strong and beautiful and joyous and gives me a sense of physical happiness.

However, our culture dictates that personal smells are offensive by definition, and so we do everything we can to cover them up. For the ancients the aromas of the body were part of a person's identity and they were exchanged as offerings. It surprises us (not entirely pleasantly) that Napoleon asked Josephine not to bathe until he returned from war. But a century earlier, in refined Elizabethan England, lovers had offered each other "love apples" as an erotic accessory. The name sounds more romantic than the fact: these were peeled apples that the lovers would lodge devotedly in their armpits and then exchange so that they would carry the essence of the beloved wherever they went.

Your smell is still a personal imprint: it changes with your state of mind and with your state of health. Anxiety, fear, stress: each has a distinctive smell. When you are sad your smell becomes almost imperceptible, as if it is as absent as your spirit. There are diseases that can be diagnosed by smell: schizophrenia produces vinegar-smelling sweat; liver failure generates breath with the smell of raw fish; diabetes smells like nail polish remover; typhoid fever smells like baked bread.

Compared to other animals, it seems, our personal smell is very intense. The intrepid Diane Ackerman recounts an anecdote about studying a bat species in Texas. To test the popular belief that these creatures love to get entangled in women's hair, she deposited one of them on her long curly locks. Far from nesting there, the creature coughed several times with disdain, flew back to its branch and spent several minutes licking itself like a cat, apparently offended by the contact.

Perhaps the human smells we find compelling are less than appealing to bats. It is probable that we choose our partners as much with our noses as with our minds and our hearts. Only today, those of us who live in the industrialized world have lost some of our natural repertoire because we live immersed in an olfactory landscape of artificial pines, lemons, roses and gardenias.

With our cleaning products (most of which contain those artificial fragrances to cover up the smell of chemicals), aromatizers to make our homes smell sweet, and the multibillion-dollar perfume industry, it seems that we just want to live in a world in which houses and people smell like flowers, fruits or enchanted forests.

It is not a question of undoing advances in hygiene and systems of waste disposal, which have done so much for our physical and mental health; but perhaps we could tone down a little the way we selectively use our sense of smell.

It could be that natural aromas beguile us in deep and abiding ways. Perhaps, as in my delayed love affair with coffee, smell does not lie but delivers—in the end—the promised ecstasy.

What emotional memories do smells arouse in you?
Our biographies are also counted in olfactory footprints. Read the list of objects and places that follows and write down the first memory that comes to you in relation to each without stopping to think. Ready, set . . . go!

- New books
- Eraser
- Shoe polish
- Freshly baked bread
- A mechanic's workshop
- A library
- Freshly cut grass
- Wet soil
- Sheets drying in the sun

OLFACTORY EXERCISES

One way to keep your sense of smell alive and awake is to exercise it daily. How?

Daily smell workout

Keep closed jars containing cinnamon, ground coffee, mint, lavender and ginger. Every morning, open them one by one and take a few short breaths from each (if you get smell fatigue, sniff the back of your hand in between to "reset" your nose). This is a way to give your nose a workout, and to keep this sense alert and alive. Stimulus and vitality live in variety.

Taking a sommelier course

With expert guidance, you can train your nose to recognize the qualities, bouquet, nuances and textures of different beverages and preparations: teas, coffee, oils, vinegars, wines, liqueurs. You could even become a professional water taster! This is a way of increasing your knowledge and at the same time refining and deepening your intimate connection with the world.

Revaluing natural aromas

Is it possible to learn to re-appreciate the natural aromas that surround you, even if they don't come out of a bottle? There are ways to perfume your house without using chemicals, such as: lighting beeswax candles; boiling eucalyptus leaves and seeds on the kitchen stove; burning natural resins like myrrh; making your own incense. You could also spread seasonal elements around your house: jasmine and lime flowers in spring; orange blossom and honeysuckle in summer; camphor seeds in autumn (they have a slight aroma of citrus and nutmeg); pine or fir needles or eucalyptus in winter.

TOUCH

Touch is the first sense that develops in a fetus in the uterus and the one that a newborn baby most explores when it arrives in the world. Just like smell (but unlike sight), touch occurs only in close proximity: it invites us to approach objects, animals and people and become intimate with them.

The organ of touch is the skin, that sensitive bubble that protects us from disease, shelters us from the rays of the sun and wards off all sorts of intrusions. It is the main part of the body that comes into contact with the world outside, but it fulfills a paradoxical role: it both separates you from and connects you with your environment. As if that wasn't enough, the skin is alive! It breathes, secretes, regenerates and metabolizes.

The skin is our largest organ and its topography registers different levels of sensitivity. The tongue and fingertips take the prize for the gift of perception. But the whole of the skin responds to touch, and when touch is lacking, it longs for it. We need to touch and be touched as much as we need air to breathe.

Decades ago it was proven that newborns who are cuddled gain weight and grow twice as fast as those who are not. In some cultures this is instinctively understood and babies are brought up in constant contact with skin. For example, in villages of the Mambuti (mistakenly known as "pygmies") in central Africa, all adults take part in the upbringing of children. Babies spend much of their time in someone's arms (not necessarily their parents'), receiving cuddles and stimuli. The Kung people carry their children in a cloth tied across the chest, in an upright position. In this way, the child can make permanent eye contact with its mother, play with her beaded necklace and see the world from her perspective. But above all it can enjoy the warmth, aroma and love of its parent 24 hours a day. It is not surprising that you never hear of colic, or kids having trouble sleeping, in these cultures.

Adulthood may be the age of autonomy, but it doesn't free us even slightly from our primary need to be caressed by someone else; this endures from our first day of life to our last. It is so vital that when there is nobody who will touch us we touch ourselves. How many times a day do we stroke our hair (women) or beard (men)? How often do we put our hands to our faces, especially when we feel sad or vulnerable? And in situations of extreme anguish, who hasn't hugged himself as if holding a baby, rocking himself rhythmically and even making soothing sounds? These caresses and simulations reminiscent of life in the uterus have a physical effect: they reduce blood pressure and heart rate, while assuaging feelings of emptiness.

In the same way, drinking a cup of tea or holding a hot-water bottle in your hands decreases feelings of loneliness. We are herd animals: everything that reminds us of one another's presence calms us down.

In a laboratory, infant monkeys separated from their mothers were shown to prefer clinging to a doll covered with soft fur but which did not dispense milk to gripping a machine made of cold metal that did deliver food to them.

In research on human beings it has been proven that if a librarian lightly touches the hand of a child while handing her a book, the child (without being aware of what has happened) will report being more satisfied with the library and the attitude of the librarian than would otherwise be the case. Another survey carried out with waitresses revealed something similar: when they made subtle and kind contact with their customers (by touching them on the back or shoulder when showing them to a table) they got bigger tips than if they didn't.

Researcher Dacher Keltner, of the University of Berkeley (California), was able to anticipate the success of a football team in the coming season by observing the degree of physical interaction between the players (how much they hugged and patted each other) as they celebrated the scoring of a goal.

Here's the best part about this simple and ancient form of human behavior: to touch, caress or massage another person is just as beneficial for the giver as for the receiver.

ACTIVITIES TO STIMULATE TOUCH

Tactile route
It is best to do this in a room you are familiar with. Close your eyes, or for maximum effect wear a blindfold. Go through the room blind, reviewing every surface with your hands and guiding yourself only by what your hands and feet perceive. It's really amazing how different a space can feel when you walk through it like this. How does the room feel at the end of the experience? More concrete? More real? More alive?

Grounding: re-rooting yourself
Also called "earthing," this simple practice consists of walking barefoot on the ground (grass, earth, sand). We are bioelectrical beings, living on an electric planet, and (with the exception of people living in cities) we are directly connected to the energy of the Earth's electrical system. In industrialized societies we rarely walk barefoot on the ground and the rubber in the soles of our shoes isolates us from its energy.

According to scientific studies, this practice strengthens the immune system, improves sleep, reduces pain, helps heal wounds and relieves inflammation.

All of our skin is a good conductor, but there is one part of it that is especially equipped to be charged electrically: the acupuncture point kidney 1 (also known as "bubbling spring"), which is located in the middle of the ball of the foot. Hence to walk or stop for a while on the earth is the healthiest and most organic medicine of all.

Choosing natural fabrics and materials

When dressing yourself or decorating your home, it is always best to choose natural materials such as cotton, linen or wool, if possible. Also make sure that your chairs and armchairs allow the body to unfold and relax as it pleases. To achieve greater stimulus to the touch you can combine different textures: the softness of corduroy with the roughness of jute; the soft texture of a cushion with the stylized lines of wood or a piece of fitted furniture. Ideally, the objects that fill your home should not only be beautiful to the eye, but also interesting, and above all inviting, to the touch.

Good questions

Gunilla Norris asks the following "questions for the heart" in her book *Simple Ways: Towards the Sacred:*

- At least once today, could I touch without a purpose or a need?
- Daily, could I caress something or someone with the awareness that I touch an inherent holiness?
- Could this day be one in which I allow myself to be defenseless for a moment in the presence of another?

SIGHT

In her treatise on the senses, Diane Ackerman says that the first creatures to experience vision were ocean organisms, as small fragments of skin sensitive to the light. As the ability to distinguish between light and darkness proved useful, the function was sharpened until it could also detect signs of movement, then shapes and finally details and colors. The origin of the sense of sight is testified to by the fact that our eyes need to be continually bathed in saline solution.

However, vision does not occur only in the eyes, but also in the brain. Otherwise we wouldn't be able to visualize entire scenes (like dreams or waking fantasies) with closed eyes.

We receive more than 70 percent of our sensory information through sight; it is with the eyes that we apprehend the world, although each of us interprets what he sees according to his own worldview. Hence the expression "seeing is believing," and the Biblical invocation "Let there be light!"

A curious fact: the eye likes novelty. We tend not to see that which is too familiar. Is that why we're so attracted to traveling, which delivers a cascade of new impressions? Can we go back to intentionally seeing what passes before us every day; even see the faces of our loved ones with "the eyes of my eyes open," as the poet E. E. Cummings puts it?

If even color occurs not in the external world but in the mind, why shouldn't we reinvent what we see and wake up every day to a new facet of our existence?

We are drawn to the light, without which vision is impossible. We are drawn to the sky. Diane Ackerman points out a fact as odd as it is irrefutable: the sky does not begin, as drawings in children's books always suggest, in some determined stratum above our heads, somewhere around the sun and the clouds. The sky begins on the ground!

We live, walk, eat and love in the sky in every moment of our lives and this sky is not merely empty space, as our eyes would have us believe: it is full of life! It continually shimmers with gases, spores, particles of earth, viruses, fungi and animals that fly up in the wind like kites. This ethereal mantle bubbles with both active flyers (insects, birds, butterflies, bats) and involuntary passengers (leaves, pollen, seeds).

And what about the feeling of lightness that the air evokes? Pure illusion. The fact is that our atmosphere weighs about 5,000 trillions of tons, and only gravity can keep it clinging to the Earth. Were it not for this force the atmosphere would float slowly and inexorably into space, taking us with it.

One last gift from the brilliant Ackerman: what if we could think of the night not as the "absence of day" but as a moment of revelation? After all, it is the point in the day when the blinding curtain of the sun is removed and we can see the reality that surrounds us: a universe of stars, planets and astonishing astral phenomena. Seen in this way, the night is a unique opportunity.

Finally, there is a difference between looking and seeing. When we look, we usually impose our own preconceptions and prejudices onto the scene so that we don't so much see what is in front of us as what we can or want to see. In *Simple Ways: Towards the Sacred,* Gunilla Norris says:

> It is a great challenge to look upon the world and be so disposed to try to see it for itself, without the layers our needs cover it with, and without the way our judgments divide the holiness of it . . . Truthfully, we cannot escape ourselves, because even in the most transparent chambers of the heart we will realize that our view is veiled. We cannot avoid this fact— but we still can nevertheless bravely turn our faces towards the world and try to see it with a loving gaze.

EYE-STIMULATING EXERCISES

Exercising peripheral vision

Look at something with a fixed focus and without moving your head or your eyes. Breathe calmly. Now try to see what is in your peripheral field of vision (to the top and bottom and on both sides). This exercise also appears later in the book, in "The Lighthouse," because it produces an immediate effect of tranquility and calmness.

Exercising the eye muscles

Bring a pencil (or other object) close to your eyes until it becomes blurred. Then move it progressively away until you see it with clarity again. Repeat the movement ten times, breathing slowly and consciously.

Looking at optical illusions

It's not just fun to play at seeing one image and another alternatively, it is also a way to remind yourself that you don't see just with your eyes, but with your mind as well. When you first look at an optical illusion you see what you expect to see (through memory, context or prejudice), but the more you allow yourself to look in different ways, the more you expand the range of possible interpretations and, as if by magic, a hidden figure appears from out of the image.

Using as little artificial light as possible
A lack of natural light can induce depression and lethargy, and a craving for sweets and carbohydrates. The ideal is to inhabit the spaces of your home according to the passage of the sun from one room to another and to delay the moment of switching on the lights as long as possible.

Good questions
(suggested by Gunilla Norris)

- Today, could I look at just one thing in freedom—without grasping, judging or denying it?
- Today, could I invite my gaze to be so innocent and simple that it shines like a lamp in the dark?

TASTE

The first food we receive is our mother's milk, and later, baby food, also from her hand. It's not surprising, then, that the association between food and the emotions is indissoluble. In adult life we continue to use food and drink to reinforce our connections with other people and satisfy our emotional hunger: we meet to have tea; we take coffee breaks together at the office; we bake cakes for each other's birthdays; we cook each other delicious things; in short, *we feed each other*.

Food and the rites that surround it have always been a fundamental part of the life of civilizations. In the past, the link we had with the food we ate was direct and primary: fruits and vegetables came to our table from our own gardens or from the orchards of friends and neighbors. Many people today seek to recover this experience by buying their food in organic markets, making their own bread or growing herbs on their balconies.

Taste is the ability to detect the flavor and reaction of soluble chemicals in food when they come into contact with the taste buds that are distributed all over the tongue. But taste is actually a more complex phenomenon involving a range of stimuli including texture, temperature, color, smell and even—in the case of hot spices—pain.

There are five basic flavors: sweet, salty, sour, bitter and *umami* (a tasty flavor, reminiscent of meat, activated by monosodium glutamate). But this is as much of a consensus as we will ever reach.

When it comes to the *good taste* or *bad taste* of food, everything is subjective. Genetics, culture and personal idiosyncrasies dictate our preferences. We are also susceptible to certain taste-bud tricks, such as that caused by an African fruit known as miracle fruit, which makes lemon taste sweet by momentarily nullifying our perception of its acid. Similarly, toothpaste can make orange juice taste bitter and chewing the leaves of the Mexican whorled milkweed plant suppresses for a while your ability to taste anything sweet.

There are some foods whose taste and texture are almost hypnotic. *Xocoatl*, for example, the original form of chocolate, is a delicious, sensual elixir made with the fruit of the cocoa tree; the Aztecs worshipped it as a gift from the god Quetzalcoatl and drank it as part of their rites and ceremonies. Today, we know that consumption of dark chocolate increases the level of the neurotransmitters serotonin and dopamine, which are associated with calm and pleasure. This may be the reason for our obsession with chocolate—although some of us favor the Aztecs' explanation, that it is of divine origin.

If food affects our emotions and urges, spices have a supreme influence on them. Not for nothing did they inspire transatlantic journeys and odysseys of a thousand and one nights. The Puritans of the 17th century understood this and denounced spices for their power to arouse lasciviousness.

For several centuries one of the most popular spices has been vanilla. It finds its way into cakes and cookies, creams and ointments, bath salts, scented candles and oil diffusers.

Like cocoa, this distinctive flavor and aroma comes from Mexico; specifically, from the seeds of the orchid known as *Vanilla planifolia* (the name comes from the fine pods through which it reproduces: the Spanish term is *vainilla*, meaning "little pod," which in turn originates from the Latin word *vagina*, literally "sheath").

The Aztecs flavored their *xocoatl* with crushed pods, which they called *tlilxochitl* (black flower). They were so highly valued that the emperor

Montezuma demanded them as tribute from his subjects. Today, vanilla is the second most expensive spice after saffron, but it is no longer exclusive to Mexico: it is grown in Tahiti, Uganda, Polynesia, Madagascar, Tongo and the Seychelles. There is only one insect, the *Melipona* bee, that pollinizes vanilla plants, but around the year 1800 the French learned to do it by hand and they established plantations in their colonies in the Indian Ocean.

It might sound incredible in this era of robots and nanotechnology: these flavors still arouse ancient emotions and reminiscences of jungles, journeys and gods.

EXERCISES TO STIMULATE TASTE

Learning to taste

We chew about 100 times a minute, but chewing isn't the same as feeling, tasting and enjoying. By putting attention into practice (we will explore this further in "The Lighthouse"), you can learn the art of savoring with a raisin (or any other food that you have at hand). How?

- Observe the raisin, turning it over to look at it from all angles, pretending that you have never seen one before in your life.
- Smell it and pay attention to whether your mouth begins to salivate with anticipation or the desire to eat it.
- Put it in your mouth. Pause to appreciate the first impression of its particular combination of sweetness and acidity.
- Allow your tongue to register its texture, which is rough and smooth at the same time.
- Chew it and notice how the flavor intensifies. Move it from one side of your mouth to the other, always giving it your full attention.
- Notice your desire, and perhaps rush, to swallow it. Swallow and feel it slipping down your throat, into your esophagus and finally into your stomach.
- Congratulate yourself for having taken the time to taste that raisin with full awareness. To give yourself the time to savor is to give yourself the time to live.

Combine herbs and spices in infusions

There is nothing like playing witch or sorcerer, creating your own formulas for tasty and medicinal infusions. Here are some combinations to experiment with:

- Chai (Indian tea): one cinnamon stick, ten seeds of cardamom, ten cloves, three tablespoons of grated ginger, one teaspoon of black pepper, four tablespoons of black tea, honey and milk to taste. First brew the hard ingredients (cinnamon, cardamom, pepper) in water for several minutes. Only add the tea as you turn off the heat, so that it does not become bitter.
- Floral tea (digestive): made with a few tablespoons of lemon balm leaves, rose petals and lavender flowers.
- Russian tea: juice of one lemon, juice of two oranges, black tea, a cinnamon stick, four cloves, honey to taste.

Make your own vanilla extract

Cut a vanilla pod lengthwise and place it in a glass jar. Fill with three-quarters of a cup of vodka, cover and let macerate for six weeks. Top up the alcohol as it goes down; all the while the vanilla pod will continue giving off its aroma and flavor. Vanilla extract is an essential flavoring ingredient in cakes and pastries.

Another option: make vanilla-flavored sugar! Cut a pod into small pieces, mix with two cups of sugar, cover and let stand for two weeks. Use to flavor and perfume desserts, and to induce sweet dreams.

Making sourdough bread

This recipe is for old-fashioned bread, made using the process of natural fermentation instead of adding artificial yeast. First you need to make a starter culture. The fermentation process is activated by combining the same amounts of water and flour (it can be half white flour and half wholemeal); covering the mixture lightly (letting in some air) and leaving it in a dark place for several days, until bubbles form. The moment in which the fermentation comes to life is miraculous, and the resulting bread even more so: crunchy crust, spongy inside, mildly acidic flavor—like the breads of yesteryear.

Once you have your sourdough starter you can make batches of bread from it forever more, as long as you continue to feed the starter daily (by pouring out some of it and refilling it with equal amounts of flour and water).

This recipe presents two challenges: you have to have a covered stainless steel pot to be able to bake the bread in and you must procure yourself large doses of patience. The procedure is simple, but you need to be available for several hours.

SOURDOUGH BREAD

900 grams of white flour   600 milliliters of water

100 grams of wholemeal flour   25 grams of salt

- For the sponge: mix 200 grams of flour, 200 grams of water and three or four tablespoons of the sourdough starter. Let it rest all night.
- In the morning pour the sponge into a large bowl and mix with 600 milliliters of warm water.
- Add the two flours little by little and mix with your hands until the flour is wet. Let the dough stand for ten minutes and add the salt.
- Knead as follows: with a damp hand, fold the dough on itself, turning the bowl around and folding four times. Continue to fold every 10 or 15 minutes (this is the only "kneading" that is required) for at least one hour.
- Divide the dough in two and shape into two balls. Place these upside down in bowls, or bannetons if you have them, and cover with floured tea towels. Leave to stand for about 30 minutes.
- Preheat the oven, with the covered pot inside, to its maximum temperature for about 15 minutes. Take out the pot, sprinkle a little flour in it and place one of the balls of dough carefully inside. Make a few incisions on top, to let the air out and improve the shape.
- Cover and return the pot to the oven. Bake for about 25 minutes with the cover on (or until the dough has finished rising) and 10 more minutes without the lid, until the bread acquires the desired color. Carefully wipe down the pot and place the second ball of dough in it, while keeping the oven hot, and cook in the same way.

HEARING

Sound connects us to the world, and the world speaks to us through sound. Even if you are alone, between four walls, there will always be some device humming nearby; some airplane that shakes the atmosphere in the distance; a car that brakes and sends you its sound waves. In space there is no sound; on Earth there is no (absolute) silence.

So true is this that acoustic ecologist Gordon Hempton has created a noise-free zone in the Olympic National Park in the state of Washington in the USA. This space is far away from roads and air traffic routes and allows you to listen to the sounds of nature without interference. In his book *One Square Inch of Silence: One Man's Search for Natural Silence in a Noisy World* (co-authored with John Grossmann), Hempton tells how he traveled around the United States recording natural sounds of all kinds until he found this quietest corner of the country and managed to get it protected by law. "Natural silence is our nation's fastest-disappearing resource," he warns.

But perhaps there is more than one way to understand the concept of silence. For designer Ilse Crawford, author of the magnificent illustrated book, *The Sensual Home*, when we talk about "silence," in reality we mean "tranquility or the absence of intrusive sounds." And this is what she recommends to her clients: that they take care to reduce acoustic pollution in their living spaces, just as they would any other type of contamination. The quality of our rest and peace of mind depends on it.

We come into the world surrounded by sounds. In the beginning, in that first watery nest, you hear your mother's heartbeat and the whisper of her breathing. This aural contact heralds a life of sound connections that are so omnipresent we barely notice them. So wrote Helen Keller, from her impenetrable silence:

> I am just as deaf as I am blind. The problems of deafness are deeper and
> more complex, if not more important than those of blindness. Deafness
> is a much worse misfortune. For it means the loss of the most vital
> stimulus—the sound of the voice that brings language, sets thoughts astir,
> and keeps us in the intellectual company of man.

Sounds don't just connect us to the voices of our loved ones, but also with the elements—the whistle of the wind, the gurgling of water, the crackling of fire, as well as with the fervent hustle and bustle of city life with its many man-made sounds.

Of course not all sounds feel the same. There are sounds that we almost universally crave—the waves of the sea breaking over the sand—and others that disturb us: the blaring of car horns, the whine of the dentist's drill, the screeching of nails on a blackboard. According to some neurologists, the almost universal reaction of shock to this last sound is explained by its association with a scream of terror.

Without a doubt, the soundtrack that we humans enjoy the most is that which we call "music," in allusion to "what comes from the muses." Music was an everyday part of life for people in the ancient world. They sang and danced to celebrate a great variety of events and thus created community, and shaped and perpetuated their cultures. They also used music to heal their ailments. Egyptian papyrus from 2,600 years ago tell of musical "spells" to cure everything from infertility to toothache.

Poetry is another vehicle to channel our musicality, through the rhythm and melody generated when words are combined. This is why poetry comes to life when it's read aloud. All you have to do is watch the posture of those who listen to it (closed eyes or a far-away gaze, body still, full attention) to appreciate the intimate, emotional, visceral impact of this spoken music in its very own rhythm.

Rhythm is especially powerful because it reminds us of intrauterine sounds. According to Ackerman, the repetitious syllables that children find easier than words when they start to talk (da-da, ma-ma) are probably evocations of the first soundtrack in the womb.

Our soundscapes may change through life, but the love of melodious harmonies accompanies us until our last day. We are musical animals as well as thinking ones and we need to make room for the melodies that lull our souls to sleep and the silences that touch and quiet our hearts and bring us peace.

EXERCISES TO STIMULATE THE EAR

Choosing the soundscape of your home
Choose home appliances that generate the least amount of noise pollution. Acoustically insulate your living space with curtains, carpets and cushions in order to reduce the noises that come from the street as well as those you generate yourself.

Singing for pleasure
You don't have to be a professional singer to be able to enjoy producing music with your voice. This form of expression is accessible to everyone, regardless of talent or being in tune. You might delight in singing in the shower or when cooking a meal. Let's go back to the habit of singing together to celebrate, honor and express our emotions.

Reading poetry aloud

Discover new poets. Read their work aloud and listen for the music it contains, which is just as important as the meaning of the words, the use of language and the concepts and images it evokes. When poetry is read aloud, whether alone or with others, it can easily become a form of prayer.

Writing poetry

If you have never dared to write poetry, there is a practice that can help you take the first step, especially if you approach it in the spirit of play. The technique is called "blackout" and was created by the author and cartoonist Austin Kleon, to free himself from a severe case of creator's block.

It consists of taking any text you have available (he used newspaper articles), choosing a topic you want to write about and crossing out anything that doesn't apply with a black pen. You will be left with a few words that you write down on a page in the form of a poem. When you read it aloud, you see what's not needed and what's missing. You keep working on your poem until you like the sound of it. It is important to do this with a playful and exploratory spirit, and to enjoy the process.

Choosing music to modulate your energy

Every culture in the world knows the therapeutic and energetic effects of music and sound. You can select songs and pieces of music to "clean" your house energetically so that you start your day with optimism and finish it calmly. Similarly, music can accompany particular moods, such as sadness (nothing helps to release tears as much as a well-chosen song) and joy (which with musical help easily becomes ecstasy).

It is important to recreate your soundtracks on a regular basis and to be faithful to the pieces and songs that touch you mysteriously, no matter how many times you hear them.

Choosing your words with awareness

In her book *Simple Ways: Towards the Sacred,* Gunilla Norris asks:

- Today, could I pause just a little moment before I speak? Might I consider whether any hasty word might limit me or someone else?
- This day, could my words be gentle and my tone full as one who has been given much? Could I be well-spoken?

Hygge, the subtle sensual charm of everyday life

Outside there is a cold wind blowing, but inside the logs crackle in the chimney. We share tea, we chat, we make confessions to each other with the relaxed confidence of those who know each other well. Nothing is missing, nothing is too much. Any luxury or accessory would be superfluous. The emotions that reign in such a situation could be listed as: connection, comfort, warmth, simplicity, authenticity, intimacy, communion, contentment.

Demonstrating an enviable power of synthesis, the Danes are able to capture all these qualities in one word (and a short one at that): *hygge* (pronounced "hu-ga") (with the "u" as in French). Impossible to translate in only one English word, *hygge* has become famous thanks to the outstanding place that Nordic countries occupy in any ranking of the happiest countries in the world. You could argue that this happiness also rests on political stability and advanced social policies, but Danish people insist that *hygge*—that ability to enjoy the little things in life—is what infuses meaning into their days and supports their well-being.

The term *hygge* can evoke an endless number of experiences—warming your hands by the fire, taking off your shoes when you get home, lying on the grass and looking up at the sky, getting lost in the pages of a book, soaking yourself in the bath by candlelight—but more than representing any specific situation it alludes to a way of experiencing. Says Louisa Thomsen Brits, in *The Book of Hygge*:

> It's a way of acknowledging the sacred in the secular, of giving something ordinary a special context, spirit and warmth and taking time to make it extraordinary.

While ultimately *hygge* is an intangible concept, it is inseparably associated with the senses. As Thomsen Brits puts it: "Hygge has a taste, a sound, an aroma, a texture . . . Do you want to make your tea more *hyggeligt* (full of *hygge*)? Add honey. A cake? Add glaze. A stew? Add wine."

What would be *hyggeligt* sounds? The tapping of raindrops on the roof, the crackling of the fire, the whispering of the wind, the singing of birds, thunder (if you are under shelter), the sighs of contentment of a person who is drawing, weaving, cooking . . . In other words, the soundtrack of a safe and familiar environment.

Hyggeligt aromas? Those that evoke fond memories for you. The smoke of a pipe; butter as it melts in a frying pan; the smell of freshly polished shoes; old books; sawdust; caramelized sugar. . .

Hyggeligt textures? Wood, wool, ceramics, leather. Rusty surfaces: organic and with a history. But not metal or glass, unless they are old.

Hyggeligt forms? Curves, because they imitate the organic forms of nature. In study after study people gravitate towards curves rather than straight lines. Curves stimulate a part of the brain called the anterior cingulate cortex, which is linked to the emotional response; by contrast, looking at sharp objects activates the amygdala, the area of the brain that processes fear.

Colors? Dark or light, but natural.

Lights? Warm, soft, intimate, that create shadows in a room and give it depth.

The quality of *hygge* is encapsulated by the familiar, the predictable, the beloved: an old sofa that has taken the shape of your body, a pile of books beside your bed, Grandma's recipes in a notebook sprinkled with flour.

Thomas Moore puts it like this in *Care of the Soul*:

> It isn't easy in our complicated world to enjoy the pleasures of ordinary living—children, family, neighborhood, nature, walking, gathering, eating together. I imagine life not as an ambitious quest, but as an anti-quest, a search for the ordinary and a cultivation of the unexceptional.

The word "simple" is key. *Hygge* quality doesn't get on well with excesses. It does not require a display of candles in the style of a Hollywood movie; just a single candle, lit at the right moment. It does not ask for a table spread worthy of an interior design magazine but a few glasses placed on a checkered tablecloth next to a vase filled with dandelion flowers.

These sensory, aesthetic and emotional qualities are imbued with the same purpose: the desire to treat yourself and others well; to enjoy a natural life, alone or in community, to need no more than what there is. The *hyggeligt* lifestyle honors the secret garden: by tending to the body, it feeds the soul.

THE RIVER
Let Your Imagination Flow

"I can't believe that!" said Alice.

"Can't you?" The Queen said in a pitying tone. "Try again: draw a long breath, and shut your eyes."

Alice laughed. "There's no use trying," she said, "one *can't* believe impossible things."

"I daresay you haven't had much practice," said the Queen. "When I was your age, I always did it for half an hour a day. Why, sometimes I've believed as many as six impossible things before breakfast."

Lewis Carroll, *Alice's Adventures in Wonderland*

Our spiritual famine has concluded—we are just beginning to restore the honor of the imagination.

Lauren Artress, *Walking a Sacred Path*

The garden leads to a meadow. We walk through tall grasses, their tips golden in the midday sun. In the distance we hear a soft murmur and we recognize the sound of running water. That is where we head. As we approach we feel a freshness that stimulates the skin and enlivens the senses. And then we see it: a bubbling brook, crystalline, flowing at a steady pace. Colorful ducks paddle across the surface, while on the bank a turtle warms itself in the sun. The waters suddenly part in the perfect parenthesis of a leaping fish. We wet our faces and our hair. At last, we give in to temptation and we slip into the water. We lie back facing the clear blue sky and let ourselves be carried away by the river.

How often have you felt like this, as if you were transported elsewhere by a magic carpet, without ever having gone anywhere at all? That carpet that takes us to unsuspected places is called "imagination" and is one of the gifts that evolution (or grace) has bequeathed to human beings.

This complex and exquisite faculty opens the doors to the past and the future, to our creativity, to a life permeated by magic and meaning, and to worlds inaccessible by any other means.

Let's look at some of the amazing qualities of this gift. Thanks to imagination you can:

- Bring to mind objects and situations that are out of the reach of your senses: for example, visualize the Eiffel Tower. You can add other imagined sensations to this image: auditory impressions (the sound of a man playing a saxophone at the base of the tower), olfactory (the aroma that wafts over to you from a nearby bakery), gustatory (the taste of a freshly baked baguette eaten after visiting the tower) and tactile (the crunchy crust of the baguette).
- Bring to mind objects and situations that do not exist in physical reality. Without much effort, you can visualize dragons, unicorns, mermaids, underwater cities and any supplementary imaginings evoked by each of these.
- Travel to the past—remembering and reliving events that occurred before the present moment—and into the future, as you plan, anticipate or dream about events that may or may not occur.

- Play at creating fantasy worlds, starting from premises such as, "What would happen if. . .?" or "Let's pretend that. . ." Play is not just for children; we adults also need this vital elixir to keep our bodies young and our hearts happy.
- Create, which means putting imagination into action in any field of life. Art is what happens when the mind plays with an aesthetic or expressive intention; but creativity can be applied to any activity: from how you dress to how you personalize a recipe that you are given. More than a human right, to create is a human need: we can't help doing it even if we try not to.
- Explore inner worlds: the universe of dreams, daydreams and your deepest intuitions.
- Visualize the inner workings of your body and influence organic processes, using your mind to collaborate with healing processes.
- Visit out-of-the-ordinary realities that are inaccessible to the senses, such as those that have been described by shamanic cultures since the beginning of time. These phenomena are not "imaginary," in the sense of being illusory, but belong to the "imaginal world," a dimension of existence known to mystics and the people of ancient civilizations who lived in the reality of visions, myths and archetypes. Australian aborigines call this realm the Dreamtime; although it is a space more than a time and they consider it more real than any empirical reality. For the French Islamist philosopher Henry Corbin, the true imagination (*imaginatio vera*) was the one that accesses this imaginal world, a kingdom between matter and spirit, in which spirits acquire bodies and bodies become spiritualized. The world of the soul.

Many people regard the imagination with suspicion, as something that has no place in adult life, but this is precisely because they are unable to understand these meanings of the word. In contrast, the wisdom traditions teach that the imagination is one of the most important, most direct channels to the divine, and probably one of the oldest. In *The Evolution of Imagination*, Stephen T. Asma, a specialist in the philosophy of the natural sciences, describes the imagination as "the eye of ancestral man" and considers it a human skill acquired before language. Thomas Moore in *Care of the Soul*, speaking from a spiritual perspective, proposes: "The key to seeing the world's soul, and in the process wakening our own, is to get over the confusion by which we think that fact is real and imagination is illusion."

Another scientist, the never mediocre Albert Einstein, defies convention when he asserts: "Imagination is more important than knowledge. For knowledge is limited to all we now know and understand, while imagination embraces the entire world, and all there ever will be to know and understand."

Let's look at some of the many ways we can explore this fantastic river and see what surprises it can offer us.

PLAY, DREAMS, MYSTERIES

Playing to Create

No child ever receives a box of colored crayons and says, "What's the point? I can't draw." Nor does she reject a jar of modeling dough because sculpture is too complicated. If you give him a guitar, he gets sounds out of it without fuss. If you ask her to sing, she doesn't refuse to because she doesn't know the words or because she hasn't got a perfect voice: she simply takes a breath, opens her mouth and belts it out!

Creativity is not just our birthright: it's the most important expression of our nature. But something happens when we begin formal education. Suddenly, to draw a tree you are only allowed to use green and brown; the sun has to be round and smiling and to be placed in a certain corner of the sky; and if you don't get it right you are told: "Look how your friend did it."

Today new teaching methods question such judgmental approaches, but for the vast majority of adults the artists that we once were have retired to winter quarters. We live in a strange paradox: as children we are dissuaded from freely expressing our creativity in pursuit of social and educational rules, and as adults we pay fortunes to free ourselves from our blockages and learn . . . to play like children!

Several artists have come to our aid. One such is Julia Cameron, who has created a rehabilitation program for blocked artists that is set out in her book, *The Artist's Way*. Cameron does not address herself only to painters and dancers, but to every living person, because there is no one born without creativity and the desire and need to use it. Cameron's main premise is that modern society has convinced us that creativity is the privilege of a few but that things were not always this way.

The Native American Tewa people, for example, do not have a word for "art" because they do not consider it an activity separate from others. Their closest approximation is *po-wa-ha* (literally, water-wind-breath), which means "the creative force that moves through all things."

Even if we accept that the creative force exists in all of us, there are some almost universal fears that prevent us from expressing it. The fears that people tell Cameron about when she suggests they should give free rein to their artistic impulses or even choose the life of an artist include: "I will end up alone and rejected by other people"; "I'll go mad"; "I'll starve to death"; and "I'll discover terrible things about myself and other people." The list goes on.

If we are to recover what we have lost we must learn to detect and (gently) silence the internal critic and encourage ourselves to let go of control, trusting that a higher force (however you conceive it, perhaps as our own subconscious) will support our efforts and show us the way. If the universe is inherently and profoundly creative, how could we—who are an intrinsic part of it—not be so as well?

Julia Cameron's
EXERCISES TO RECOVER YOUR OWN VOICE

Writing your morning pages

Actually, you can write them at any time of day, but the morning is best because it allows you to channel the energy of your dreams, and also because the effect continues for the rest of the day. The aim is to write three pages by hand, without stopping to correct or edit yourself, and without reading what you have written (until you finish working through the book).

This stream-of-consciousness writing frees you from the mental noise that gets between you and your intuition and creativity. In the pages you will see yourself thinking, dreaming and holding a dialogue with yourself. Many pearls may turn up in the course of your writing (interesting images, insights you were not aware of, possible projects), but the point is not for these pages to be somewhere to fish for items to be used elsewhere but to give your mind permission to express itself freely. The idea is not to seek to channel the river but to learn to let it flow.

A date with the artist

Spend two hours a week on a "date" with your inner artist. This can mean visiting a museum, seeing a play, walking around in the park, going to an antique shop or just sitting down in a favorite coffee shop to read or write. The only two conditions are: go alone in order to focus on the guest of honor—the inner artist who languishes for lack of attention—and don't use this time to do anything you are obliged to do. At the end of the date, note down how the experience went.

Write three parallel lives (that you would have liked to live)

The idea here is to think without limits. Write about yourself as a pilot, Arabian dancer, monk, carpenter or soap opera actress. Once you have done that, notice which "autobiography" brings a smile to your lips, or a glint to your eye, by merely reading it. Think of a gesture or action that you can incorporate into your day, to take you in the direction of fulfilling your longing. It can be purely symbolic.

Strive for balance

Draw a circle and divide it into six "portions," as if it were a pie. Put the following labels on each area: work, exercise, fun, friends, romance/adventure and spirituality. Draw a point on each portion to indicate how satisfied you feel in that sector: closer to the outer edge means greater satisfaction. Connect the dots. This drawing will show you where you feel there is something lacking. Are there any simple ways that you can nourish neglected areas? Do this exercise every now and then and observe whether the drawing becomes more harmonious and balanced.

Exploring Your Dreams

The same rationalist judgment that dismisses the imagination also regards dreams as unimportant. Many people are convinced that they do not dream. The truth is that we all have four to six dreams in an eight-hour night, lasting approximately two hours. Other people remember their dreams, but do little or nothing with them, for lack of tools and motivation. After all, what do these fading night movies matter when they evaporate like soap bubbles the moment you wake up?

The first records of dreams date from 5,000 years ago when they were inscribed on clay tablets in Ancient Mesopotamia. The Greeks and Romans read messages from their deities in their dreams, and in many cultures dreams are considered to have prophetic meaning.

What are dreams? In the simplest definition they are a succession of images, ideas, emotions and sensations that we experience while we sleep. Science regards them mostly as a mechanism of mental processing that helps the mind update its beliefs, memories and perspectives. From another point of view, they are a fertile territory for the expression of the unconscious and a mirror that can help you to understand your deep motivations, and the fears and longings that you do not allow into your conscious mind. In the shamanic worldview (as we shall see shortly) they are conduits to realms of non-ordinary reality, which you can turn to for information, healing or guidance.

The language of dreams is not easy to understand because it is metaphorical, working in the same way as imagination and poetry. Its logic does not know time or space. In a dream you can be alive and dead at the same time; you can be a child and an old person; you can change sex, or you can fly or cross worlds in an instant.

Is it necessary to know how to interpret dreams in order to be able to relate to them? No: you can also receive their gifts with the soul and the heart, without a clear intellectual comprehension. This is precisely what the Jungian psychoanalyst Jill Mellick proposes in her book *The Art of Dreaming: Tools for Creative Dream Work*. Mellick invites you to establish a creative link with your dreams, allowing their imagery to inform and inspire your conscious mind. After all, she says, good books and films also leave us with images we don't understand and yet they move us: "Even a film in an unknown language can touch something universal in the depths of the heart."

The challenge is to approach dreams as if they were a foreign language that you need to approach with respect, subtlety and a lot of curiosity. This way of working with dreams differs from traditional methods in several senses: instead of interpreting, explore; instead of identifying, imagine; instead of categorizing, connect; instead of learning, allow yourself to wonder at mystery; instead of simplifying, be enriched by the experience; instead of seeking to understand, appreciate.

The Greek word *psyche* means "butterfly" and also "soul." Dreams give wings to the soul, says Mellick, but only if you hold them as you would a butterfly: with an open palm and in silence. If you try to pin them down with categorical interpretations, you may have a greater sense of control, but your dreams will no longer fly.

EXPLORING DREAMS NON-ANALYTICALLY

In order to explore your dreams, you need to remember them! Keep a notebook and a pen (or cell phone, for recording) next to your bed, and write down or record what you remember —it could be a word, a color, or an image—before you get up.

Incubate a dream: before going to sleep, tell yourself: "Tomorrow I'm going to wake up clearly remembering what I have dreamt of," without pressure, knowing that the suggestion may take several days to take effect.

To get inspired, talk to other people about dreams or read up on the subject.

Choose three words to amplify

The Jungian method of "amplification" differs from that of Freud's "free association," in which you are encouraged to gallop from one idea to another, gradually moving away from the original image. In amplification the dreamer barely moves away from the concept and quickly returns to it, weaving a web of meanings around it. How is it done? Write a word (or image, or idea) that has appeared in your dream and begin to draw arrows in all directions towards the different words or images that the original concept evokes. Then draw more arrows connecting each of the new words so that a sort of spider's web of images appears. Observing the complexity of this growing web will bring you closer to the richness and depth of your dream images.

Make an energetic drawing

Keep blank sheets of paper and crayons, pencils or markers handy near your bedside. When you get up, after writing down the essence of the dream close your eyes and relive it mentally, evoking the emotional tone and the feelings in your body. Open your eyes halfway, choose a color and, using your non-dominant hand, imagine that you are breathing the energy that you feel through your arm to the hand holding the pencil or crayon, and express the sensations passing through you on to the paper. You can also use both hands simultaneously. The focus must be on evoking the images or the energy of the dream, and exhaling them onto the paper. Don't look at the picture that is forming. If necessary, turn the sheet over or continue on another one as the energy you are evoking flows. At the end, write the date and a title on your sheet of paper. Meditate briefly on the drawing, without judging or analyzing it.

Absorb the energetic drawing back into your body

One way to meditate on the finished drawing is to "translate" it back into the language of the body through movement, sound and emotion. Place your hand on the drawing and, as if you were reading Braille, imagine that your fingers can translate the color and the line into sound. Let the vibration of the forms rise through your arms up into your throat and come out as sound. You may feel like making loud, shrill sounds to denote high or thin lines, or deep guttural sounds corresponding to thick lines or those at the bottom of the page. The instruments that translate the lines into sound are not your eyes but your fingers. In this way you can recover the energy of the dream, relive it and transform it.

Omit parts of the dream, as if removing pieces from a puzzle

Once you have written down a dream, you can try taking away images or fragments from it while asking yourself: "What quality would be missing from the dream if this part weren't there?" Make two columns on a piece of paper, one with the images that you have removed, the other with the quality that is missing as a consequence. For example, suppose you dream that you are traveling with an old Indian woman in the back of a car, on your way to a ceremony. If you take away the image of the old Indian woman, the feminine wisdom would be lacking; if you remove the fact of going to a ceremony, the sacred purpose would be missing; if you eliminate the traveling in the back of a car, the notion of being carried, and of destiny, will be absent.

Turn a dream into poetry

Write down your dream in narrative form. Divide it into stanzas. Remove all unnecessary words. Add punctuation marks. Add new images that occur to you as you do so. Give it a title. Read it as if it is in a book of poetry and see what emotion this produces.

Hang your dream in a museum gallery

If an image appears in a dream that attracts your attention and you are intrigued by it, you can imagine it enlarged to a huge size and then hung on the wall of a museum. Visualize yourself standing in front of it, looking at it. What thoughts and feelings does it evoke?

In the same way you can turn a dream into a *haiku* (a form of Japanese poetry), mask, sculpture, myth, map, mandala, dance, performance, fairy tale, collage or . . . anything else that your imagination wants to bring forth. If there is one thing that helps when learning a new language, it is to be daring!

Active Imagination

But we don't just dream when we are asleep. The mind is constantly weaving positive and negative scenarios in the form of things like fantasies and worries, into which unconscious images and content intrude. What if you could create these dreams at will, by establishing a fertile, transformative dialogue with your own unconscious? Below are some exercises to help you do just that.

The active imagination is a technique created by the father of depth psychology, Carl Gustav Jung, to put the self in direct contact with the unconscious, while all the time being aware of what it is witnessing. "The active imagination must be understood as a way or method to heal, elevate and transform the personality," explained Jung.

A key to the exercise is not to try to manipulate or twist what appears, but merely to observe it and allow it to mutate by itself into other images or forms. This exercise can be done via silent meditation or through writing, painting, or any other technique of self-exploration.

Jungian author Robert A. Johnson develops this technique in his book *Inner Work: Using Dreams and Active Imagination for Personal Growth*. He tells stories of patients who were able to rely on this technique to solve psychological problems, heal wounds, fulfill previously unviable desires and even live rich parallel lives, giving symbolic form to energies that were seeking expression. The therapeutic power of active imagination lies in the participation of the ego, which dialogues with the unconscious as an intentional and independent force.

How do we know that the images that appear are gifts from the unconscious, not creations of the ego? Because unconscious material often surprises us, expressing archetypal and transpersonal motifs (see "The

Mountaintop" later in this book), and sometimes even frightens or disconcerts us. The sensation is that of watching a film that you are not creating yourself.

NB: this exercise is not suitable for people who have difficulty distinguishing between reality and fantasy or between the reality of this inner world and the reality of the outer world. It is a powerful technique, and for some people it could be destabilizing.

Another warning before we begin. It is essential to respect personal ethics and values—yours, if you are working by yourself, and those of anyone else involved if you do this work in company—when working with the imagination. Inner experiences are real to the mind and have an effect on the psyche. Also, it is necessary to continue to attend to relationships and obligations in real life. Active imagination is a fascinating tool but it cannot and must not replace our experiences in the real world.

PRACTICING THE USE OF ACTIVE IMAGINATION

Invite the unconscious to participate

Do this lying down, in a quiet place, where you won't be disturbed. It may help to play soft music in the background. "The active imagination requires a dream state, halfway between sleep and alertness," wrote Jung. Take some deep breaths and relax your body progressively. Start by asking, for example: "What am I worried or obsessed about at the moment?" "Where does this emotion come from?" "What is the image that represents it?" Remain silent, with your eyes closed, and wait for an image to appear on your mental screen. Sometimes it is difficult to make this happen on the first attempt. The idea is to wait patiently for it to manifest and, when it does, to not try to change it or manipulate it: just observe it, and see how it changes by itself.

Engage in dialogue with the image

This can be done in a meditative state, without opening your eyes, or you can record the exchange on paper (or on a computer). Ask a question, wait for the answer to appear and write it down without questioning it. Then ask another question. The idea is to give symbolic form to the usually ungraspable contents of the unconscious and thus to narrow the gap between it and your conscious mind.

Honor what happens with a ritual (see "The Fire")

To perform a symbolic action that brings the experience into the world, so as to inscribe the information received and to let the unconscious know that you are listening. For example, if the message the image gives you is that you are too rigid with yourself, you can perform a gesture of openness and flexibility.

Traveling between Worlds

Tens of thousands of years ago the people of the Earth conceived the world as a place inhabited by spiritual intelligences: the spirits of nature, called, variously, fairies by the Celts, *kontomble* by the *dagaras* of West Africa, *apus* by the Incas; and tribal ancestors and ascended teachers. They communicated with these intelligences through a set of practices universally known as "shamanic." The name seems to come from the term šamán in the Tungú language, spoken in Siberia. It means witch doctor, or literally "the one who knows." There is, however, an alternative explanation that places the origin in a Sanskrit word for mendicant monks in India, *śramana*.

From the beginnings of human civilization, almost all the peoples of the Earth have used some variant of the practices that Romanian anthropologist Mircea Eliade baptized "techniques of ecstasy" to heal themselves, to communicate with spiritual forces and to ask their gods for help.

What is new today is that people who have grown up in industrialized urban cultures are now exploring these practices for themselves with the help of experienced guides. They seek to reconnect with ancestral forces; heal ailments that conventional medicine cannot treat; glimpse realities not perceptible with the senses; and confirm sensations and intuitions for which they cannot find an explanation.

One of the great facilitators of this approach was the American anthropologist Michael Harner, who in 1980 summarized and detailed the common elements of the world's shamanic practices in his book *The Way of the Shaman*. Among these shared elements, Harner highlighted three in particular. The first of these is the state of shamanic consciousness: a kind of trance, but one in which the practitioner does not lose consciousness or control. The second element is the shamanic journey, usually accompanied by the rhythmic sound of a drum or maracas. Thirdly, shamanism is predicated on the belief in a non-ordinary world that can be divided into three parts:

- The Lower World, inhabited by ancestors, power animals and forces of nature;
- The Higher World, inhabited by beings of light and spirits of wisdom and compassion (although these can also be found in the Lower World);
- The Middle World, inhabited by people and disincarnate (disembodied) spirits. All the realities of the human world belong to this dimension of existence.

In traditional shamanic cultures only the shaman "travels" anywhere. Modern neo-shamanic practices make such journeys available to anyone willing to learn the techniques, but the process must always be guided by someone trained in shamanic arts and familiar with the worldview that sustains them. I am not going to suggest any neo-shamanic exercises here, out of respect for the tradition of passing on such ancestral knowledge in person.

Still, the question arises: is it legitimate for people who do not belong to these traditions to make use of their techniques? Harner says:

> . . . these new practitioners are not "playing Indian," but going to the same revelatory spiritual sources that tribal shamans have traveled to from time immemorial. They are not pretending to be shamans; if they get shamanic results for themselves and others in this work, they are indeed the real thing. Their experiences are genuine and, when described, are essentially interchangeable with the accounts of shamans from nonliterate tribal cultures. The shamanic work is the same, the human mind, heart and body are the same; only the cultures are different.

But, he warns, shamanism requires a commitment to learning:

> In shamanism, the maintenance of one's personal power is fundamental to well-being . . . The techniques are simple and powerful. Their use does not require "faith" nor changes in the assumptions you have about reality in your ordinary state of consciousness . . . However, while the basic techniques of shamanism are simple and relatively easy to learn, the effective practice of shamanism requires self-discipline and dedication.

Practices associated with the exploration of this worldview are: the shamanic journey; singing; dancing; praying; ingesting psychoactive plants (called "entheogens" by the communities that use them, meaning "a god within"); sweat lodges; and vision quests, which involve spending time alone in nature, fasting and communing with the spirits of the place.

The deep imagination

Bill Plotkin, who is the founder of the Anima Institute, comes close to describing shamanism when he proposes "the deep imagination" as a way to comprehend the voice of running water, the murmurs of fire, the song of a landscape and the language of every kingdom that inhabits the Earth. Plotkin explains:

> Deep imagination is a translator, fluent in the languages of animal and plant, canyon and star, wind and stone, as well as the languages of our own depths—the expressive modes of nature and soul being essentially the same. But, to be clear, this is not a one-way path, for imagination not only allows us to receive, but to offer as well. We rely upon imagination for our own expression, for our own communication across these same frontiers. Imagination is central to our own capacity to participate meaningfully with the rest of creation in bringing forth the world. And, the rest of creation is longing for us to participate in this great dance in our individual unique ways—through the embodied life of our souls.

The active dream

After undergoing a series of transformative mystical experiences, the Australian author Robert Moss created his own synthesis of shamanic practices with Jungian active imagination. His methods offer the possibility of exploring non-ordinary reality as part of a group and in a spirit of play and adventure. His proposals include group "re-entry" into a particular dream in order to look for information, healing, resolution or simply to get to know the dream world better. Other group activities include conscious dream journeys to predetermined locations, accompanied by a drum; and "navigation by synchronicity."

Synchronicity is a concept coined by Jung to describe the occurrence of two events united by meaning and not by causality. Examples of this include a book falling into your hands with the exact information you were seeking; or hearing the same foreign-language word three times in a single day, and finding it significant to the moment you are living. Although this phenomenon occurs spontaneously, Moss likes to purposefully encourage it. One way is to play at reading the world as if it were an oracle.

ACTIVE DREAM PRACTICE

The street oracle

Before leaving home, formulate a question for which you would like to receive guidance or orientation. The first three things that attract your attention in a specific time frame (your journey to work, a walk around the block, a trip on public transport) will give you the answer. You may be drawn to a captivating headline, overhear a fragment of conversation, notice a phrase on a billboard or be fascinated by a formation of clouds in the sky. The oracle will tell you what the hidden message is in this succession of "random" images.

The group oracle

Each participant in a group writes down a phrase that comes to mind on a piece of paper. Alternatively, you can open a book at random and pick the first sentence on the page. Pile the pieces of paper on top of one another, face down, in the middle of the group. One by one, each participant asks a question and takes one of the papers at random. The phrase she reads on it is the answer to her question. In some cases, the answer will be clear and synchronous; it is likely to be so astonishing as to awaken a sense of mystery. In other cases, it will be necessary to use the imagination to figure out the relationship between the question and the answering phrase. Ultimately, everyone benefits from looking at their question from different angles, thus foregoing our usual, linear style of thinking.

Dream transfer for healing purposes

This exercise requires two people. It can be done with groups divided into pairs. The two roles should be alternated so that everyone experiences both sides.

Person A describes an aspect of his physical or emotional health that requires healing. Person B closes her eyes and asks her unconscious for a dream (an image) that will serve as a threshold for healing A's condition. B tells A about the image. A takes the image and "enters" it with the help of the drum, to explore it for himself.

Visualization

This technique is as simple as it is powerful. It has been used for many decades for diverse purposes: to alleviate pain; to combat anxieties, phobias and other psychological ailments; to counteract addictions; to improve mental and physical performance; and to prepare for potentially stressful situations. The name is somewhat misleading because visualization really involves all the senses, not just sight, and is experienced with the whole body, not just the mind. In fact, only 55 percent of people find it easy to see images with their eyes closed. Another name for this technique is "guided meditation."

What does it consist of? It is a self-induced trance, similar to self-hypnosis, and it can be done in several ways: following directions given by another person (live or recorded); following a memorized script; or improvised.

The effectiveness of visualization rests on the intricate connection between the body and the mind, and the fact that the mind cannot distinguish between scenes that you imagine and those that you experience on the physical plane. A good visualization can communicate positive, healing or motivating messages to your unconscious through images, sensations and symbols. Mobilizing unconscious processes for conscious objectives, and doing so in a state of relaxation, maximizes the chances of a successful outcome. There are studies showing that guided meditation can have an effect even when you're asleep.

This technique potentially offers many health benefits. Less than ten minutes of guided meditation can reduce blood pressure, cholesterol and blood sugar levels. Other effects observed have been an increase in the activity of immune system cells, faster repair of fractures, better healing of burns, a decrease in bleeding and a reduction in the need for post-operative pain medication. Beyond physiological responses, the use of guided meditation can improve state of mind, quality of life, emotional health, intuition, abstract thinking, creativity and empathy.

According to psychiatrist Belleruth Naparstek, a pioneer in the development and application of this technique, there are three principles that help to enhance the effect of visualization.

- **Provide detailed sensory information and powerful emotional stimuli.** Sensory images are the language of the body, and the body understands them perfectly. For a swimmer hoping to improve her performance, for example, the best practice is not just to imagine herself winning the race, but to become aware of how her body feels as it enters the water at full speed, the pressure of the strokes, how the air comes into and out of her lungs every time she pops her head out of the water and the sound of the applause at the end of the race. To add emotion, she could also conjure up her father's smile and the inflection of his voice as he congratulates her on her first triumph.
- **Generate an altered state of consciousness.** The induced semi-hypnotic state of a visualization alters brain waves, mood and awareness of time and cognition. This multiplies the chances of achieving the desired outcome.
- **Produce a sense of control.** Medical literature reveals that when you feel a sense of mastery and control over your experience, this in itself is therapeutic and helps you to feel good, and to boost your optimism, self-esteem and ability to tolerate stress and pain. Visualization makes you feel in control because it is the result of a positive action that you take for yourself.

GUIDED VISUALIZATION PRACTICES

In his book *Imagery for Healing, Knowledge and Power*, William Fezler suggests starting by creating a hypnagogic state, one of profound relaxation, to enhance any visualization that comes subsequently. Below is a simplified version of his induced relaxation practices.

Simplified relaxation practice

Sit comfortably and start counting from one to ten, telling yourself at every step that your eyelids are becoming heavy and that your eyes are very, very tired. Tell yourself: "The heavier my eyelids feel, the more relaxed I am and the better I will be able to follow the suggestions that I make to myself." Count to three, close your eyelids and allow your eyes to roll backwards for a few seconds. Then think: "My eyelids are now so heavy that I doubt very much that I can open them." You will begin to feel a wave of pleasant relaxation in your feet that rises slowly up through your body. As the wave advances, every part of you will go to sleep. Keep counting as the relaxation ascends to the top of your body. From time to time repeat the suggestion about your eyelids. Finally, when your whole body is sleepy, say: "On the count of three, my whole body is going to be completely relaxed, completely in a state of rest." One . . . two . . . three . . .

You can then go on to create any visualization, or simply enjoy the state of deep rest and calm you achieved.

The forest scene

The following is a visualization that incorporates the entire range of possible perceptions of the five senses. In addition to creating a state of relaxation, this sensory activation brings a feeling of joy and vitality. It will also lower your pleasure threshold and make you more prone to positive emotions. This is the suggested script:

You are walking through a forest of pine trees on a beautiful summer day. See that the sky above is brilliant blue. Feel the warmth of the sun on your face. Hear the soft, low rustle of the wind through the pine boughs. Blue jays fly from branch to branch, sounding out in loud, high cackles.

Reach up and pick a pine needle. Break it in half. A drop of fluid falls from the needle onto your hand. Sniff the drop. It smells of bitter pine. Lick the drop. Taste the bitter flavor of pine. Now you come to the edge of the forest. Pass into an orchard of apples, brilliant red in the sunlight, against deep green foliage. Pick an apple. Take a jackknife from your pocket and slice the apple in half. Beads of apple juice sparkle on the metal of the knife blade. Sniff the sweet scent of apple. Carefully lick the juice. Sweet taste of apple. Next you pass into a grove of lemon trees, yellow fruit in chartreuse leaves gleaming in the summer sun. Pick a lemon. Peel it. Smell the sour flavor of the rind. Bite into the lemon. The sour juice squirts into your mouth. Your cheeks pucker, your saliva flows, as you suck the lemon juice. And you continue walking.

Come out of the lemon grove onto a sandy ocean beach. Dazzling turquoise water stretches as far as you can see. Smell the salt in the air. Lick your lips. You can taste the salt from the ocean spray.

Walk out into the hot, dry sand. Move closer to the shimmering sea, standing on the wet sand. Remove your shoes and socks. Feel the cold, wet sand beneath your bare feet.

Walk back up on the beach. Strip down to a bathing suit. Lie down on the warm sand. A gentle breeze begins covering you with sand. Feel it light and dry, coating your body. Feel the ever-increasing pressure as the sand continues to cover you, dry, heavy sand. Safe, secure, protected, in a warm cocoon of sand.

Now the sun is setting on the ocean. The sky is a throbbing orange, turning fiery red on the horizon. As the sun sinks into the water, you are enveloped in a deep violet twilight. Look up at the night sky. It's a brilliant starry night. The sound of the waves, the taste and smell of the salt, the sea, the sky, and you; and you feel yourself carried upward and outward into space, one with the universe.

Imaginary worlds. Envisioned kingdoms. Dreaming journeys. Active reverie. We know so little about the mysterious experiences that explode like fireworks when we close our eyes. Perhaps the only thing that matters is that which the poet Mary Oliver expresses with her enchanted pen:

> Whoever you are, no matter how lonely,
> the world offers itself to your imagination.

We go to the river for pleasure, curiosity, need and thirst of discovery; and we return transformed. Before we depart, let's listen to the advice of the girl from Wonderland, Alice of the blond locks and white apron. She calls to us before setting off to chase after some impossible creature: "I nearly forgot," she says. "You must close your eyes, otherwise you won't see a thing."

THE MOUNTAINTOP
Tell a New Story

Mythology helps you to identify the mysteries of the energies
pouring through you. Therein lies your eternity.
Joseph Campbell

What you can plan is too small for you to live.
What you can live wholeheartedly will make plans enough.
David Whyte

The climb is hard going. There is no shade or place to rest in sight and the route is steep. So steep that the only thing we see is the rock wall that we are conquering through pure tenacity. We continue upwards, all our attention fixed on the next step. After a long while, before we can realize what is happening, we make it to the summit! The sky is within our reach; the air is clear and transparent; and we have a bird's-eye view of the world that spreads out downwards in all directions, like a flowing multi-colored dress. Distance, height, freedom . . . How different everything looks from this vantage point!

It is easy to get perspective when you are high up, but what we really need is to be able to access such vision and clarity while we are living below on the plain. Above all, we need this perspective to navigate the rocky sections of our journey, as we skirt outcrops and craters and abysses. What could provide us with the necessary distance to be able to see life with clear sight? What could be the metaphorical peak on which we can stand in order to look down? Here is one answer: learn the language and the poetic wisdom of myth.

Let's start at the beginning.

WHAT IS A MYTH?

A myth is a story that human beings tell themselves in order to explain what the world is and how it works; what life is; what death is; our duties and obligations; how we should treat each other; and what to make of the things that happen to us.

The lives of our forefathers were steeped in myth. Told around the fire, passed down as an inheritance from generation to generation, these were not just compelling tales: they encapsulated important information about the origin of the world; they helped people to find true north and gave them guidance to make vital decisions.

No one has done as much to convey the importance of myths as Joseph Campbell, author of *The Hero with a Thousand Faces* and *Reflections on the*

Art of Living, the Masks of God series and many other wonderful books. Campbell's writings provide Western society—gripped by the illusion of unlimited economic and technological development—with a set of deeper insights. His explorations ranged from literature and psychology to anthropology and language; but his focus was always on his beloved myths. With unparalleled lucidity he taught his readers to interpret these primal stories in a metaphorical way and invited new generations to feed on their ancient wisdom—which remains undiminished, despite the somewhat archaic language.

According to Campbell, myths serve four basic functions:

- The first function of myth is mystical: to teach us to embrace life in both its marvelous aspects—pleasure, beauty, joy—and in its monstrous aspects—suffering, disease, death, the need to kill in order to eat. Myth shows us how to respond to what comes our way, not begrudgingly or with resignation, but with awe and gratitude.
- The second function of myth is cosmological: to explain the laws of the universe in a manner that makes profound sense to us.
- The third function is sociological: to establish and validate a certain social order, giving each person a sense of belonging to his particular tribe.
- The fourth function of myth is educational: to teach us how to pass through the different stages of life; how to be a child, teenager, adult, father/mother, grandfather/grandmother; and eventually how to grow old and how to die. For Campbell this was the most relevant of the four functions, as it shows us what it means to live a good life.

From the creation myths of the Earth's original inhabitants; through Greek, Egyptian and Babylonian myths; the Ten Commandments; the Torah of the Jews; the *Bhagavad Gita* of the Hindus and the Noble Eightfold Path of Buddhism; all wisdom traditions offer stories that lead human beings by the hand from the first to the last of their days.

This way of understanding and living life has lost credibility to such an extent that today the term "myth" is used as a synonym for "lie." It is as if an account that is not factual has to be a falsehood. People who hold this opinion of myths do not understand that they are, in fact, metaphors; they are truths born of the soul and narrated in symbolic language. As the fourth-century Latin thinker Sallustius remarked, "Now these things never happened, but always are."

Today, we no longer learn about life through myths, but from science, which does not directly address questions of meaning. To a certain extent, this function is satisfied by poets, musicians, film-makers and artists of all kinds. As Campbell puts it: "It would not be too much to say that myth is the secret opening through which the inexhaustible energies of the cosmos pour into human cultural manifestation."

There is a reason why all sorts of artistic and cultural creations—the *Star Wars* saga among them—have been inspired by Campbell's interpretations of myths.

But these works do not reach everyone equally, nor do they manage to cover the full spectrum of the needs of our psyche. In the absence of effective communal myths, we need to construct personal myths to light our own way.

Because our lives are greatly influenced by the power and the quality of the stories we tell ourselves, it is important to make regular climbs to the summit, to look down on our problems, paths and decisions through "mountain eyes."

PERSONAL MYTHOLOGY

In 1963 Jung began his biography, *Memories, Dreams, Reflections*, with this confession:

> Thus it is that I have now undertaken, in my eighty-third year, to tell
> my personal myth. I can only make direct statements, only "tell stories."
> Whether or not the stories are "true" is not the problem. The only question
> is whether what I tell is my fable, my truth.

What, then, is a personal myth? It is the particular combination of stories, beliefs, images and symbols that make up your vision of the world.

Our ancestors did not have the opportunity to examine the myths that guided them. They could not see beyond them; much less question them. Modern civilization extols *logos* (reason) over *mythos* (the pattern of images and beliefs of a culture); it privileges linear understanding over narrative and provides us with the necessary distance from our own conceptions to see them as such. The idea is not to discard or change our stories every time life becomes difficult. It is more about adapting the story: replacing rigid and dysfunctional myths with ones that are more flexible and life-giving.

"A belief traps us or frees us," says physician and therapist Rachel Naomi Remen. For example, the belief that the majority of people are unreliable creates a life high in adrenaline and gives very little social sustenance. A worldview that holds the contrary view—that the majority of people are 100 percent trustworthy all the time—is dangerous.

A more moderate and realistic belief—that most people are sincere and well-intentioned, but that there are also confused people who can do harm—provides a narrative that allows you to flourish: to live with an open heart, but without denying your capacity for judgment and discernment.

Our personal myths evolve over our lifetime. Some of the myths that have governed us in the past may have had their *raison d'être* but may now be dysfunctional and obsolete.

In Stanley Krippner and David Feinstein's book *Personal Mythology: Using Ritual, Dreams and Imagination to Discover Your Inner Story*, they give two examples: in one, a girl learns to win her parents' love through academic success. As an adult she continues with the same strategy, obsessively pursuing professional achievements. But the love she longs for never comes.

In the other, a teenager develops a rebellious personality in order to survive his authoritarian parents. The same myth in adulthood condemns him to live recklessly, repeatedly losing jobs because he sees a threat in every authority figure.

In both these cases, a pattern that was functional in one moment of life becomes an obstacle to personal growth later on.

A large part of our emotional suffering originates in living with myths that are not aligned with our needs, potentials and circumstances in the present. We need to become aware of these unconscious beliefs in order to discard those that no longer serve us or represent us.

Sam Keen, author of *Your Mythic Journey: Finding Meaning in Your Life Through Writing and Storytelling*, suggests: "Rewrite your autobiography every ten years. Telling our stories may be the most human thing we do. By telling stories we remember our past, invent our present and envision our future."

EXERCISES FOR LEARNING TO TELL A BIGGER STORY

In order to change a myth, you have to start by recognizing it. Here are some ideas inspired by the writings of Krippner, Feinstein and others:

- Examine the myths that predominate in your family of origin. Write down in a few words what was thought or said in your house about: success; obligations; money; relationships; body image; and about right and wrong. Read what you have written, as if it were someone else's text. Do you agree with these notions? How far are you honoring these beliefs in the choices you make in your life today? Which of them do you consciously choose to adopt? Which ones do you need to discard completely? Which ones are still valid, but require updating?
- Look closely at the iconic figures you admired in childhood (characters from books, movies, cartoons, or people you knew in real life). Are there any clues in these role models to the kinds of myths you aspire to incarnate? Is there any trace of these aspirations in your life? Would you still choose these same role models?
- Tell the story of your life in the third person, starting with the classic "Once upon a time. . ." Name the protagonist—you can choose a generic title such as "the prince," "the princess," "the orphan girl," "the young hero," or an invented name. What is the protagonist looking for? What is her greatest longing? What are the obstacles that stand in her way and how do they help her find her strengths? What is the genre of the story (tragedy, comedy, mystery, romance. . .)? What's the next chapter? If it were a novel, a play or a movie, what would it be called?

Once you have understood the myth by which you have been living until now, you can create a new mythical vision, reinventing your own myth, following the steps outlined as follows:

- Identify the myth that wants to be born. Let's take the example of Peter, who wants to leave his position in the company where he has worked all his adult life and try his luck as an entrepreneur. He is tired of following someone else's rules; tired of doing the same work day after day; and tired above all of not being able to change his life. The new myth will need to be inspired by a vision of courage, freedom and self-determination.
- Identify the conflict between the old myth and the new. In Peter's case, this is the desire for adventure and excitement (new myth) versus the safety and comfort (old myth). Understand both visions, without judgment.
- Create a new vision that integrates the parts of the old myth that are still active with the emerging myth. The path of evolution does not require abolishing previous states of belief, but including them in your new worldview while at the same time transcending them. You don't discard the knowledge you learned in primary school when you move on to high school; you build on it. In our example, Peter could try to honor the stability that the old myth provides by looking for some modest form of income, so that he can take the leap to the new myth without so much anguish. It could be that this plus point of the old myth—the preservation of a certain sense of order—becomes part of the new myth.
- Refine the new mythical vision. Do all possible to start living from it.

The more effective your guiding myth, the better equipped you will be to meet life's challenges. But changing one's myth is not only a matter of understanding, but one of courage and bravado. The kind of courage and bravado that is a hallmark of the Hero's Journey.

THE HERO'S JOURNEY: THE GREAT STORY

Joseph Campbell, the great mythologist mentioned earlier, dedicated five years of his life to studying and comparing the mythologies of the world. After a long and exhaustive exploration, he came upon a conclusion that captivated him: whatever the locations for the stories, the characters featured and even the languages they were told in, all the myths shared the same basic structure. He found the same pattern reflected in Siberian,

Ona, Yanomami, Nordic and Aztec myths, and also in other story genres such as fables, legends, fairy tales, sacred texts, movie plots and works of literature. Campbell called this monomyth, or universal story, "The Hero's Journey."

Why is this script so omnipresent? Because it gives an account of the path of growth and evolution that each of us undertakes in life. We travel this route not just once, but many times: every time we need to take an evolutionary leap. The Journey is a play in three acts: the call, the initiation and the return.

The call

The hero is living his normal life in his town or village when something happens that forces him to leave the known world behind. It may be that the king gets sick and the hero must go in search of the healing elixir; or someone disappears; or there is a famine that threatens to decimate the village. Another form of the "call to adventure" is when an animal runs through the village and the protagonist can't help but follow it, only to get lost in the deep forest. There are also some heroes who start out on their own, driven by pure thirst for adventure. (I speak of "heroes" here, and not "heroines," for reasons to be explained shortly.)

The challenge of this stage is to answer the call. When the protagonist ignores the call, the consequences are catastrophic. In psychological terms, the call is an impulse of the psyche to grow; and if the ego resists, out of fear or unwillingness to step out of its comfort zone, there is a price to pay in the loss of vitality, direction and meaning. A kind of "living death" ensues that can only be resolved when the resistance is overcome and the journey begins.

The initiation

The journey always requires the protagonist to leave their familiar environment and go on a quest for something, in uncertain and dangerous places: a treasure hidden at the bottom of the sea; a temple at the top of a mountain; a secret kept in the heart of the dark forest. These scenarios represent the threshold or transition point common to all heroes' journeys: the hero has left the known world behind but has not yet reached a new destination. This state of uncertainty occurs over and over again in life, especially when something in your environment collapses (a relationship, a job, the death of a loved one), and brings with it a state of fear, confusion, grief or anguish.

The hero faces trials and challenges, but he also encounters allies. In fairy tales the ally may be a leprechaun, a fairy, or an old sage who offers him a talisman, a potion or some magic words that will be his lifeline when he encounters a certain challenge further down the road. In Campbell's words, this ally figure represents "the benign, protective power of destiny." In other words, the ally is your intuition that assures you that when you summon up courage and respond to the call, life will provide you with clues to confirm that you're on the right track. Then the final battle can be fought and the hero achieves his victory: he gets the treasure; kills the dragon; discovers the truth he sought. Transformed, he sets off back home.

The return

The return is not without challenges. The hero may not want to return from his destination at all. Sometimes, what he finds is so wonderful that he is tempted not to return and prefers to stay in that magical world for ever. In life this can happen when you fall in love. When you have found the "magical other" you lose interest in everything else except being with that person, and it can be tempting to turn your back on your old life and obligations. It can also happen to the artist who fears rejection and keeps his art—the treasure he has found—to himself, as a mode of protection. This is a negative detour: in fact, the journey calls you to return, to bring back the bounty you have found and to offer it to the community.

THE HEROINE'S JOURNEY

For women the journey may take a different route, as theorized by the Jungian psychologist Maureen Murdock in her book *The Heroine's Journey*. In her clinical work, she explained to me, as well as in the experiences of her friends and herself, she repeatedly comes across a different story from that of the hero. In it, she detects what she calls "a wound in the feminine."

What is this wound? It is the separation from feminine qualities that happens to girls trying to live up to an ideal expected of them by the masculine culture and values that predominate in most modern-day societies. Today, women are asked to undertake the same journey of external conquest that has always been demanded of men if they are to compete in the professional marketplace. Women who are determined to succeed find themselves sacrificing, at an early age, qualities such as receptivity, sensitivity, empathy, intuition, compassion and creativity. At a certain point along the way, many of them wake up, look around and wonder if all that they have achieved (status, recognition, wealth) has not come at too high a cost. They may not regret what they have achieved, but they feel a completely different hunger: a desire to be still, to breathe, to respond to their passions and, ultimately, to find a means to channel the yearnings of their soul. Having answered the question, "What am I capable of doing?", another query now appears as an insistent whisper: "What do I *want* to do?

Faced with this malaise, many women embark on a second journey. If the hero's journey is onwards and upward, the heroine's is inward and downward. Murdock says:

The hero's journey is focused on the adventures: slaying the dragon, finding the boon, meeting the goddess. For the heroine, the first part of the journey is the separation from the feminine, because of the focus in our culture on the idealization of the masculine. The individual in a patriarchal culture is driven to seek control and power over themselves and others; still slaying the dragons, internally and externally, and finding the boon, more externally. But for women, this doesn't feed our nature. We ask, "What happened to my desire to write, to paint, to dance?" And then, we experience the descent. So, there's a split when we focus more on making it in the world, rather than on listening to our deep self.

When this second, later-life journey takes place, it often manifests as a vocation for "universal motherhood": a dedication to healing, nurturing or sheltering some segment of the world in need of care. The conclusion of this second journey is the integration of the feminine with the masculine in a synthesis of forces that archetypal psychology calls "the sacred marriage."

In this quest women are not alone: men correspondingly go in search of the feminine that is part of them. This reintegration of the two facets of a human being is one of the most urgent needs of society today. This is how the Sufi mystic Llewellyn Vaughan-Lee, author of *The Return of the Feminine and the World Soul*, puts it:

As we awaken from the repression of the patriarchy we need to reclaim the sacred feminine, both for our individual spirituality and for the well-being of the planet. Our ecological devastation points to a culture that has forgotten the sacredness of the Earth and the divine mother, as well as denied the feminine's deep understanding of the wholeness and interconnectedness of all life.

In the personal life of men there is also a thirst for the soul; and the soul has always had a feminine quality. As Vaughan-Lee puts it: "The ancient female figure of the soul of the world, the spiritual presence in creation, unites one's own individual path with that of the world."

Although we arrive by different paths, our reward for the journey is the integration of opposites. The true longing of the soul is never at odds with the desires and needs of the community. To discover our purpose and to have the courage to pursue it is the task of heroes and heroines alike.

WHAT IS AN ARCHETYPE?

But what are we talking about when we talk about "heroes" and "heroines"? Certainly not comic-book heroes, or people who perform heroic deeds full time. We are really speaking here of the "archetype" of the hero or heroine. Plato, the fifth-century Greek philosopher, was the first to use this word to refer to the perfect forms that lie behind the many manifestations of the physical world. Thousands of years later, Carl Jung amplified the concept to include an idea, image or pattern of behavior that is present in the collective unconscious.

What this means is that although no one has explained to us that these forces or patterns exist, we recognize them when we see them and feel their power when they come to life inside us. These energies are represented by an endless number of characters in literature, and we run into them every day in the street, in the office and in our own inner experiences. Or, as Campbell eloquently puts it in the opening pages of *The Hero with a Thousand Faces*: "The latest incarnation of Oedipus, the continued romance of Beauty and the Beast, stand this afternoon on the corner of 42nd Street and Fifth Avenue, waiting for the traffic light to change."

We can, for example, cite the 12 essential archetypes that Jungian author Carol Pearson explores in *Awakening the Heroes Within*. These are: The Innocent, the Orphan, the Warrior, the Caregiver, the Seeker, the Destroyer, the Lover, the Creator, the Ruler, the Magician, the Sage and the Fool. Each one incarnates a particular constellation of qualities and a way of being in the world.

We need to be able to draw on this range of resources at various stages of life, and even at different times of the day. It is important to be able to be a good boss when you're at work and have a team to lead, but you need to know how to take off that "suit" when you sit down for coffee with a friend. When you get home to your waiting children, you may want to get in contact with the Caregiver's nurturing ability, or the gift of the Fool for being whimsical and silly. Similarly, if someone threatens your children, or anyone else you hold dear, it will probably bring out the ferocity of the Warrior—even if you normally find it difficult to give a strict order to a poodle.

It is important to clarify that these roles do not strictly correlate with gender. Pearson says:

> Some women tend naturally to be Warriors and Seekers, and some men to be Caregivers and Lovers in spite of their cultural conditioning. The point is for both to take their journeys in such a way as to find their own way to be male or female, and eventually to achieve a positive kind of androgyny, which is not at all about unisex, neutered behavior, but is about gaining the gifts both gender energies and experiences have to offer us.

So what do you need to know about these characters you carry inside yourself? What would it be like if you could observe them in action, in yourself and in others, and you could establish a conscious link with them, so as to be able to bring out the best they can offer you as and when you need it, effectively *acting out* their parts? Conversely, if you ignore their presence, it is very possible that they will be the ones *acting through you*. It is a very different thing to choose to fight for a good cause, or to know how to channel your inner warrior when appropriate, than to be surprised by an outburst of violence from within that you didn't even know you were capable of. It's not the same to deploy your loving energy consciously, contacting the Lover within, as to become a serial seducer.

It's good to know that we can all be heroes, that we can all be wise, that we can all be creators at any given time; but that no one is *the* Hero, *the* Sage, *the* Creator.

The more roles and energies you have available, the richer your life will be. If you have been acting, say, as an Orphan or an Innocent or a Caregiver up until now, it's important that you know that, because you are human, you have a much greater range of possibilities at your disposal.

A Beautiful Question

One of the most effective ways of rethinking your life and looking at it in a broader context is self-inquiry. The already-mentioned Sam Keen, who used to give personal mythology workshops with Campbell, likes to say that his main spiritual practice is precisely that of asking questions. Not just any question, of course, but "the great mythical questions which can never have definitive answers."

"Always the beautiful answer who asks a more beautiful question," wrote the poet E. E. Cummings. Here are some beautiful questions suggested by Keen:

Questions to ask on your own journey

- Where am I going?
- What is my life about?
- What do I value?
- What gives me a sense of purpose?
- What is sacred, meaningful, of ultimate concern to me?
- What are my deepest longings?
- Where am I now on my life journey?
- Who gave me the map I have followed thus far?
- Who defined success and happiness for me?
- Have I forgotten the adventure I once planned, the dreams that guided me?
- When I get bogged down, nearsighted, lost in the details of making a living, how do I find my way out of the forest?

Mythologist Dawna Markova also provides questions aimed at illuminating areas of life in which new myths might be wanting to emerge.

Questions to ask to find out what new myth wants to be born

- In your current life, what are you being a voice for?
- Who or what are you serving?
- What is it too soon for, too late for, or just the right time for?
- What brings beauty into your life right now?
- What are you valuing?
- What are you drawn to in others?
- How would you have answered these questions in the past?
- How would you like to be answering these questions in the future?
- In what areas of your present reality are you finding security?
- In what areas are you taking risks?
- What aspects of yourself are hiding or dormant?
- What are you studying?
- What are you teaching?
- What are you cultivating?
- What is expanding in your life right now?
- What is contracting?
- What would you like to be?
- What is the connective tissue of your life right now?
- If your heart could speak right now, what would it whisper to you?

The invitation of the mountain summit is to see with new eyes, but also to act accordingly. Once we know that a greater life awaits us, we must walk resolutely in the direction of that challenge.

For decades, Campbell taught at Sarah Lawrence College in the USA, when it was exclusive to women. When he started teaching, most of his students had no other ambition than to find good husbands and become good wives. With his words he inspired them to dream bigger, and in turn they helped him—through their heartfelt questions—to turn his lofty ideas into wisdom for use in everyday life. To them, and to anyone else who responded to his plea but felt they lacked the courage to follow suit, he dedicated these words of encouragement:

> We have not even to risk the adventure alone for the heroes of all time have gone before us. The labyrinth is thoroughly known . . . we have only to follow the thread of the hero path. And where we had thought to find an abomination we shall find a God. And where we had thought to slay another we shall slay ourselves. Where we had thought to travel outwards we shall come to the center of our own existence. And where we had thought to be alone we shall be with all the world.

THE SWAMP
Embrace Your Shadow

If you bring forth what is within you,
what you bring forth will save you.
If you do not bring forth what is within you,
what you do not bring forth will destroy you.
Gospel of Thomas

Who has seen a shadow separated from its light?
Rumi

The emerald-green carpet stretches around the trunks of the oaks and the poplars, inviting us in. We place a confident foot on it, and it sinks. Before we have a chance to think we take another step, and it follows suit. Suddenly we get it: the ground was no ground at all, but water covered with floating plants and mosses. Before we know it, we're knee-deep in the swamp, and the more we struggle to get out, the deeper we sink. Everything indicates that we will be here for a good while. Where did we take a wrong turn on the path, to get stuck in this predicament?

The answer is: nowhere. The swamp did not appear in our path because we went the wrong way; it is a feature of the landscape that we will have to cross again and again as we move through life. Its waters are not treacherous; they just take us by surprise. That is the nature of this part of our psyche that Carl Jung called "the shadow."

While Sigmund Freud had already begun to explore the concept of the shadow, Jung (who was his disciple before breaking ranks) added layers and depths to it. He also attributed positive and creative aspects to it, and gave it a different status by conceiving it as one of the main archetypes of the collective unconscious.

WHAT IS THE SHADOW?

It is the collection of psychic contents that we don't want to, or cannot, admit into our conscious minds. How does this phenomenon arise? Let's see.

We all come to this world *whole*. As babies, our psychic apparatus does not yet distinguish between objects, forms, people, the self and the world. But we do not take long to develop this capacity, and so we are thrown into a world of dualities.

The process of acculturation cements these distinctions, forever separating good from evil, valuable from valueless, the beautiful from the horrifying. We soon learn that we can do or say things that awaken love in our parents and earn their validation, and things that provoke their anger and disapproval.

In his *A Little Book on the Human Shadow*, poet and essayist Robert Bly says that, as we grow up, the rejected parts of us are thrown into a bag that we drag behind us. As children, when we hear admonitions like "don't do that," "don't say that," "don't feel that," and tenets such as "girls don't yell" and "boys don't cry," then emotions such as anger, frustration and grief, as well as a host of impulses, desires and feelings of all kinds end up in that heavy backpack.

Bly remembers that when he and his twin brother were 12 years old, in their hometown in Madison, Minnesota, they were known by the nickname of the "nice Bly boys." "Our bags were already a mile long," says the author. In addition, the prohibitions and instruction that *create the shadow* don't just come from the adults in our lives, but also our peers and, in time, ourselves.

The emotions that tend to be in the shadow are the afflictive or painful ones, but into the bag also go qualities that were simply not "available" to one person because they were the domain of another family member ("My sister is the talented one," for example), as well as those that could reveal a family secret or upset a delicate social balance (such as curiosity or rebellion). In the same way, men can hide (from themselves and others) their feminine aspects, and women their masculine ones.

Therefore, the bag also contains the "golden shadow," as Jung called the positive qualities or gifts that we have not had the permission or the opportunity to develop, or even recognize as our own. For example, someone might not pursue his musical vocation because he grew up in a family that valued sporting or intellectual achievement over everything else. Another person may not be able to feel or express tenderness in adult life because toughness was admired and respected in her family; or her capacity for joy may have been stifled by an environment that prioritized seriousness or even melancholy.

Nonetheless, most commonly our backpacks overflow with difficult emotions (sometimes misnamed "negative") such as fear, anger, sadness, guilt, shame, jealousy, envy and resentment. As Argentinian psychologist Norberto Levy explains in his seminal book *La sabiduría de las emociones* (*The Wisdom of Emotions*), these emotions have nothing to do with negativity. They are highly functional warning mechanisms, which point out to us what is missing, or affecting or worrying us; and they give us the opportunity to correct it. For example, anger delivers the news that something or someone has transgressed some important boundary.

Fear warns you of a perceived threat that you believe you don't have the resources to deal with. Sadness reflects a loss (past, present or future) that demands your attention. Envy is the sudden and painful remembrance of a lack. These emotions are uncomfortable for us, and expressing them often exposes us to some degree of social disapproval.

Depending on our upbringing, some emotions will be easier for us to feel and express than others, and so we will hide those that embarrass us behind others that are more acceptable. Thus anger can pose as sadness; an "inappropriate" desire can be disguised as anxiety; resentment about being asked to do something we do not want to do can manifest as guilt; hostility can be turned into fear; and "I don't want to (do something)" can appear as "I can't." Similarly, repressed self-affirmation can see the light as passive-aggressive behavior; inhibited sexuality can show up as puritanism (or, at the opposite extreme, as disturbed sexual behavior) and repressed tenderness can mutate into misogyny (or the rejection of any form of sensitivity or vulnerability).

Occasionally, these shadowy emotions and qualities may be expressed virulently. It is important to understand that this is not so much a reflection of the intrinsic depravity of the original emotion as of the force of the repression that the ego exerts. "The shadow is only dangerous when you don't give it due attention," according to Jung. And also: "Everyone carries a shadow, and the less it is embodied in the individual's conscious life, the blacker and denser it is."

What consciousness avoids, the body displays, so our shadows also present themselves in the form of physical symptoms (teeth-grinding, stomachaches, headaches), psychological traits (guilt, phobias, neurosis, depression, obsessions) and neurotic behaviors (self-inflicted accidents, bad decisions, self-sabotage).

PROJECTION: A KEY MECHANISM FOR DETECTING THE SHADOW

One of the main mechanisms through which the shadow expresses itself is projection. What does this mean? It means transferring to another person some aspect of your own psyche or personality that you can't see, recognize or accept; in other words, that you can't own. This perception generates a strong—positive or negative—reaction in you, but without you recognizing it as originating in yourself.

For example, if you are driven and hard on yourself and you see a woman sunbathing in a square on a weekday you may get irritated and think: "How can she be so lazy?" If you find it hard to express anger, you might be outraged by people who have no problem enforcing their boundaries. If you have parked your self-esteem in your shadow, you might be irritated by someone who recognizes his own virtues without reservation. If you have your feminine qualities in your shadow you might have an unconscious aversion to women or, conversely, a disproportionate admiration for women who are stereotypically feminine (and the same the other way around, if it is your masculine attributes that are in the shadow).

This mechanism creates false enemies and pushes us away from people. We do not see individuals as such (complex, multifaceted, unique), but as representatives of some group: "the boastful," "the frivolous," "the vulgar," "the authoritarians" and such. This kind of blanket condemnation can also fall upon a collective: artists, hippies, rich people, members of a certain race, affiliation or culture.

Some anthropologists even speculate that what we consider "evil" could be the result of our natural aggressiveness driven underground by an excess of civilization; in other words, by the repression of our inner wildness. However, Jungian analyst Marie-Louise von Franz cautions that indigenous or native peoples have shadow elements of their own, such as self-determination, individuality and freedom of thought. The fact is that everything that has substance has a shadow.

An extreme case of projection is the so-called "witch-hunt." This begins when a person or a section of society rejects and disowns some dark feature of their psyche, which no one ever lacks completely: for example, *Schadenfreude*, which is the pleasure caused by a rival's misfortune; an inappropriate sexual appetite; or some relatively innocent but somewhat twisted or wayward impulse or desire.

Ken Wilber, the creator of integral theory, points out:

All of us have a dark side. But "dark side" does not mean "bad side";
it means only that we have a little black heart ("There's a little bit
of larceny in everybody's heart"), which, if we are fairly aware and
accepting of it, actually adds much to the spice of life."

According to the Hebrew tradition, says Wilber, God placed these
dark whims in the hearts of men to prevent them from perishing from
boredom. To which we could add that they also make our value judge-
ments and decisions mean something. What value would the effort to be
good have for us if goodness were our only option?

A witch-hunt happens when a powerful group of people—or an entire
society—feels a pressing need to deny certain impulses. They cannot admit
that these impulses exist in themselves and that they demand expression.
A sequence is then established: they believe that they don't have these
impulses but yet they feel them manifesting, and so they conclude that
someone else must be responsible for them. It becomes urgent to find and
eliminate the possessor of the "little black heart" through a witch-hunt.
Without outside offenders to blame, they would have to face the fact that
the troublesome emotions are their own. At the same time, the recipients
of the projection (the targets of the witch-hunt) are constant reminders
of the loathed quality or impulse, and so become even more repulsive.

The danger posed by this level of repression is evident in the many
persecutions groups of people have suffered throughout history: the
Roman persecution of Christians; the Salem witch trials; the Ku
Klux Klan's victimization of African Americans; the extermination of
Jews in Nazi Germany; the perpetual harassment of minority groups,
such as homosexuals, and of traditionally disempowered sectors of the
population, such as women.

At a more mundane level, this proclivity appears in the everyday,
"innocent" love of gossip. The "little black heart" beats in delight when
whispered criticisms do the rounds, and it will continue to do so until
we are willing and able to see it for what it is. Where there is hatred,
prejudice, irritation or enjoyment in the berating or diminution of a
person or group, we need to suspect that the offensive trait belongs, in
some measure, to the one calling it out.

We spend the first twenty years of our lives deciding which parts of
our psyche to put away in our bags, says Bly, and the rest trying to lighten
the load. The truth is that your shadow is always looking for you: it

presents itself spontaneously in dreams, in the art that you produce, in verbal faux pas, in inexplicable behaviors. Each time such things happen you are offered a fresh opportunity to see your shadow, re-own it and neutralize its negative charge.

The first contacts with your shadow can be, at the very least, disturbing. If your reaction to any of the following exercises is anguish, it will be beneficial to address whatever comes up with support from a good therapist. You can also explore the shadow's contents with the help of a trusted friend or work with a group. The important thing is to freely choose the best way for you. "My mind is a neighborhood I try not to go into alone," confesses writer Anne Lamott.

A word of caution: don't imagine that you can empty your bag once and for all; it is in the nature of the psyche to create shadow as it moves through life. But if you dare to wade into the waters every time something weighs on you, obsesses you or tightens your guts, you will be practicing the best emotional hygiene possible and you will be able to keep the swamp from overflowing.

Not only that: to be conscious of the swamp makes you whole, dependable, genuine and free. Jung said: "One does not become enlightened by imagining figures of light, but by making the darkness conscious. The latter procedure, however, is disagreeable, and therefore not popular." This unpopular task may be the most transformative adventure of your life.

EXERCISES TO RECOVER QUALITIES FROM YOUR SHADOW

Exhortations

The ancient Greeks engraved two maxims in the temple of Apollo at Delphi: "Know thyself" and "Nothing in excess." Both are exhortations to observe and recover your shadow. A way to detect projections is to look for the excesses to which you are inclined: what irritates you in particular (that does not necessarily irritate others) in a way that you can't explain rationally. Or, at the opposite extreme, what dazzles you or obsesses you in the people you admire (a sign of the golden shadow: positive qualities that you cannot yet recognize in yourself).

Once your particular "excess" emotion has been identified, you can ask yourself to what extent those qualities might be present in you, albeit in a milder version. In the examples mentioned at the beginning of this section—from laziness to boastfulness—the lesson may not be that you should dedicate your life to loitering, or be forever drawing attention to yourself, but that you need to give yourself permission to rest, or to recognize your gifts and your value without false modesty.

3-2-1 process

This procedure, recommended by Ken Wilber and his fellow authors in Integral Life Practice, is a three-step method of undoing the projection by which we unconsciously transfer our own undesired qualities onto another person.

Here is an example of how projection can alienate uncomfortable psychic content from a person's mind:

1 An employee is angry at her boss. She can't very well stay angry, because harboring or expressing anger might put her job in jeopardy.
2 She unconsciously projects her anger onto her boss; and now she thinks that *it is her boss* who is angry.
3 In a further effort to protect herself from the disturbing emotion, she might experience it as a second, inauthentic emotion, such as sadness, that takes its place; thus, in her mind, she is not angry, she is *depressed*.

The projection is now complete: the anger went from herself, to her boss, to no one at all. It has "successfully" been removed from her consciousness, and from the world. Only it has not, and it will continue to affect her in disguised form.

This is the procedure recommended to undo the projection:

Step 1 Describe the situation. For example: X irritates me because he is envious and competitive. He always needs to be noticed and that drives me crazy.

Step 2 Converse with X, in an imaginary exchange in writing. For example:
Me: Why are you always looking for attention?
X: I barely share anything of all that I want to share. Why does it bother you?
Me: It's not necessary for everyone to know everything about what you do...

X: Why not? Who am I hurting?
Me: I think we all need to be more humble. . .
X: Who says that sharing or showing what you do isn't humble? And who says we all have to be humble?

And so on, until the root of the conflict reveals itself.

Step 3 Assimilate into yourself the quality that is causing the conflict:
"I am also competitive and I would like to be able to emphasize my skills and qualities from time to time, so that other people can acknowledge and admire them."

The first reaction to this last step is usually discomfort (after all, this is precisely the quality you were trying to hide from your consciousness).
But, if you persist and relax in the face of this discomfort, usually the feeling that arises is one of relief, and liberation. You have just regained a little piece of yourself.

In an abbreviated version, you can ask yourself last thing at night, before you go to sleep, "What caused me to react in a disproportionate way today? What irritated me? Or what fascinated me?" In this way you can start to reclaim what you have expelled from your consciousness that day.

Working with your projections can rouse resistance, but eventually you will feel like you have put down something heavy that you were carrying. You will feel less wooden and constrained, more human, more complete. And the best part is that you will be able to use the energy you have freed up to do something new and creative.

FROM MANDALA TO MANDORLA

We have already said that very early on in childhood we learn to see life divided into "positive" and "negative" events and phenomena—light–dark, health–disease, good–bad, life–death—and to favor the former, as if we could erase unwanted qualities at a stroke.

To make matters worse, we tend to think of these opposites as contradictory (white–black, top–down, right–left) instead of as *complementary*. If they really were contradictory, we should be able to draw a clear dividing line between one and the other. Who can point out the precise moment that day becomes night, or health becomes sickness?

In *Owning Your Own Shadow: Understanding the Dark Side of the Psyche*, the Jungian analyst Robert A. Johnson points out that Westerners are pulled in different directions by two sets of opposing values: secular and religious. The first includes values such as doing, winning, receiving, deciding, possessing, eating, having sex. The second covers the complementary opposites: being, foregoing, giving, obeying, lacking, fasting, abstaining.

When you choose one set of values at the expense of the opposite, you violate your own integrity. "The mistake," says Johnson, "is that we have forgotten the original meaning of the term 'religion': *re* (new) *ligare* (unite)." In his words:

> The religious faculty is the art of taking the opposites and bringing them back together again, surmounting the split that has been causing so much suffering. It helps us to move from contradiction—that painful condition where things oppose each other—to the realm of paradox where we are able to entertain simultaneously two contradictory notions and give them equal dignity. Then, and only then, is the possibility of grace, the spiritual experience of contradictions brought into a coherent whole, giving us a unity greater than either one of them.

Through paradox we can understand the sacred value of giving, and also the need to receive; the need to do, and the need to rest in being. Knowing that we need complementary opposites enables us to understand that if we tilt the scales too much in one direction, we must make a movement (even if it is symbolic) in the opposite direction, to restore balance.

If contradiction condemns us humans to dissociation, paradox is a dance that creates space for mystery and vitality.

In another book, *Living Your Unlived Life: Coping with Unrealized Dreams and Fulfilling your Purpose in the Second Half of Life,* Johnson gives us a perfect image to summarize the healing nature of paradox.

Today almost all of us have heard of the mandala, a symbol from India and Tibet that represents wholeness with its circular shape and clearly demarcated center. We are less familiar with a related symbol of Western, specifically Christian, origin: the mandorla.

A mandorla (which means "almond" in Italian) is an oval frame in the shape of a *vesica piscis* ("bladder of the fish"), a symbol comprised of two interlocking circles, representing the union of opposites, often containing the figure of Christ, the Virgin, a saint or a prophet; they were much used in Romanesque and Byzantine art.

Here is what it symbolizes: a mandorla represents the union of heaven and earth, good and evil; life and death come together in it, offering the spectator the mystical experience of unity or integration. "When the most Herculean efforts and the finest discipline no longer keep the painful contradictions of life at bay, we are all in need of the mandorla," suggests Johnson.

His book offers exercises on how we can use this image in our lives.

EXERCISES FOR INTEGRATION

Uniting polarities

- Choose a dichotomy in life that you want to work on. For example: work and leisure, love and power, responsibility and spontaneity.
- Take a sheet of paper and on one side draw an image that represents one of the two poles of your chosen dichotomy.
- On the other side of the sheet of paper draw the opposite pole. If you catch yourself getting self-conscious about your artwork, try drawing with your non-dominant hand. The important thing is to let go, not stop to think.
- Notice how the two polarities confront each other from opposite sides of the paper. Imagine how those images could blend together or combine.
- On another sheet draw some form of interaction between the images on the two sides. It could be a clash, a dialogue or some kind of communication at a distance.

- On a third sheet allow the dialogue to continue to evolve. When an image of synthesis emerges, observe the soul state that gave birth to it. Then reflect on how this new image might manifest itself in your life.

Ritualizing conflict

You can pay tribute to qualities that usually go unheard through a small symbolic act. Johnson recalls the case of a couple he used to counsel, who couldn't stop arguing heatedly at the weekends. After analyzing the causes of their unresolved discord, Johnson prescribed the following exercise.

They were to begin each Saturday with a ritual: they would meet each other in the living room at a scheduled time, greet each other with a bow and then spend ten minutes giving free rein to their animosity, hitting each other with foam rubber sticks. At the end they had to bow to each other once again, put the sticks away in the closet and begin their weekend. Holy remedy!

The couple were finally able to enjoy their time together in peace. What was the explanation for this magic? It has partly to do with the power of ritual (see "The Fire", p. 157) and partly to do with making space for the warrior energy that crackled between them but had been channeled in unconstructive ways. The rite was a way of paying a tribute to Ares, the Greek god of war and one of the many incarnations of the Warrior archetype.

Honoring the disowned

Another way to integrate our opposites is to choose a quality from the list of "unwanted" emotions or behaviors and find some way of expressing it, without causing damage or disturbing the contrary quality. How? By dancing it, writing it into a story, burning it or burying it—however you want to symbolize it. For the psyche, a symbolic act can have the same weight and impact as a physical one.

In the long run, we must learn to live in a world of dualities and to accept that from time to time we will once again find ourselves in the sticky waters of the swamp—just when we were beginning to think we had reached solid ground. Don't despair! Each time this happens is a fresh opportunity to roll up your sleeves, sink your arms into the mud and uncover the treasures that lie hidden there.

Like a wise grandfather from across the millennia, Rumi whispers:

> What hurts you, blesses you.
> Darkness is your candle.
> Your limits are your quest.
> You must have both a shadow and a light source
> Listen and rest your head under the tree of recollection.

THE VILLAGE
Deepen Your Relationships

Love never dies a natural death.
It dies because we don't know how to replenish its source.
Anaïs Nin

If anything other than love could do it
I'd have done it already
and left the hardest for last.
Stephen Levine

You may have tackled the ascent to the mountaintop, the mud of the swamp, the forest or the river. And now you come upon a different territory. The wind brings children's laughter, barking dogs, chinking glasses, voices raised in debate, declarations of love. We walk towards these sounds and come to the gates of the village. We dry the sweat of our brows as we cross the threshold with a firm step, our hearts hungry for human contact. We are home, at last!

Here, among friends, parents, children, partners, bosses, neighbors, is where everything happens. The most sublime joys and the most arduous pains and disappointments. More than once we are going to want to run away, back to the peace of the mountain, to the serpentine flow of the river, to any place where we feel immune from these difficulties. But we will return, again and again; because the village calls, as life calls, and we can't help but answer.

Like dogs, horses or dolphins, human beings are gregarious animals from the first breath. But while other species court, mate, raise their young and share their lives on instinct, the bonds we establish as human beings are of a psychological and emotional complexity unmatched by the other inhabitants of the planet. We are able to dedicate decades of our lives to educating our children; to create amazing organizations to take care of our sick, elderly and needy; to risk our lives in order to save perfect strangers from death—and also to band together to inflict unimaginable cruelties on each other.

If love is the force that makes the universe go round, why is it so difficult to simply love each other?

TO BELONG AND TO BE ONESELF

"There is no force other than love in the world," wrote Rainer Maria Rilke, and then, "for a person to love another person—this is the most difficult task of all." Did the poet contradict himself? Not exactly: he was talking about two different planes of reality. On the one hand, the absolute love that mystics, poets, wisdom traditions and spiritually minded consciousness researchers extol as the ultimate substratum of existence. And on the other, the challenging scenario in which we weave our bonds here on earth (the world we perceive ourselves as living in, known in Hinduism as *māyā* and thought to be illusory), in which every expression of love is partial by nature and only occasionally evokes the splendor of its source.

We yearn for a perfect love that fills our bodies and souls, but we fight over trifles, distrust each other and act in ways that sabotage any possibility of quenching our thirst.

Is it an irony of fate? In our darkest times it is easy to think so. But this much is true: as in fairy tales, it is in the dark cave where the gold is hidden. Approached with awareness, it is exactly our relationships with other human beings—even as they fail, change, or challenge us—that can most effectively propel our personal growth. This is what John Welwood, among many others, asserts. The brilliant American psychologist, author of books like *Love and Awakening*, and *Perfect Love, Imperfect Relationships: Healing the Wound of the Heart*, will lead our explorations in this territory.

When Welwood's first marriage ended in divorce, he focused on examining how it was possible for a relationship between two people who genuinely loved each other to fail. He wanted to explore the ways to develop, in his words, "an awakened, conscious relationship."

He found no answers in his meditative practice or in the teachings of Buddhism, of which he was an adept, because they illuminated the absolute plane of existence and took little interest in the world of dualities and relativity. Nor did he find what he was looking for in his profession (Western psychology), which explores connections between people but mostly ignores the source of unconditional love—of a spiritual nature— from which our failed and limited relationships feed. After a long search he finally realized that what was needed was a profound and intelligent dialogue between these two approaches to knowledge. Where they meet, he reasoned, a praxis was possible that could honor the absolute nature of love along with its relative manifestation in our relationships (and in our personal history). The perfect could interact with the imperfect; the finite with the infinite.

From a broad perspective we can think of love as a combination of openness, warmth, attraction and desire for connection that unites us with each other, with the environment that surrounds us and with life itself. We all recognize this state because we have lived it. We know that, when we experience that delightful joy that intimacy brings, there is no need to seek the meaning of life, or even to ask ourselves what the word "love" means, because we feel it with every cell of our being. Let's see how.

As we explored in "The Swamp," you come into the world in a state of entwinement with the whole. Your mother's arms, the light that filters through the curtains, the air that caresses your skin . . . Everything is fresh, captivating, astonishing and, at times, unsettling. Sensations follow one another without the mind yet being able to capture them in thoughts and stories. But that state of openness is not free from needs. We need milk; our skin begs for touch; our eyes seek out a devoted glance from our caregiver; our nervous system requests stimulation; our tiredness cries out for rest.

English psychiatrist Donald Woods Winnicott postulated that a child has two basic needs: contact and space. On the one hand, he or she needs to be seen, caressed, acknowledged, received; but children must also have time and space to explore the world for themselves, without interference.

THE FIRST WOUND

Both needs are unfulfilled to some extent because perfect parents do not exist. There are parents who are tired, mistaken, distracted, frustrated; parents who harbor their own unsatisfied emotional needs or who unwittingly project them onto their children. From very early on we develop some degree of frustration: we want Mom to show up and she doesn't; we ask for one thing and get another; we want to continue exploring our toes and instead we get passed around from one pair of arms to another as a bunch of strangers try to make us smile.

We can also speak of an even more primal wound, of a spiritual nature, which is caused by our separation from the whole at the moment of birth, when we incarnate as individual beings apparently severed from the web of life. From a biological point of view there's a third reason for our vulnerability: we human beings are born with a terribly immature brain that will take many years to finish forming into a state that will allow us some degree of autonomy. Until that process is complete we remain helpless, entirely dependent on the goodwill of the people in charge of us.

What happens to that radiant sun that shines in the middle of our chest when it comes up against these "affronts" of the world? It hides behind a mantle of clouds. As we grow, the ego—that psychic structure through which we recognize ourselves—generates a diverse array of clouds, in the form of: defenses, limiting beliefs, distrusts, unconscious programming, traumas and afflictive emotions such as fear, jealousy, anger and resentment, which become part of your personality and drive you daily further away from your own heart.

Then, when you come across someone who sparks your affection, your defenses melt and you feel as if the sun comes out in your innermost self. The other person and her qualities—beauty, goodness, sense of humor, capacity for astonishment, tenderness, joy—awakens in you an absolute love. And in this state—at its most intense when you are in love—you perceive the light of your own heart in the radiance of the heart of the loved one.

However, opening up to your romantic partner brings you face to face with your own vulnerability. Inevitably, at some point the other says or does something that makes you uncomfortable, hurts you or sparks your anger, reminding you of the pain of your primal wound and covering the inner sky with a thick layer of clouds. Immediately, old thoughts begin to awake from dormancy: "I am unlovable," "I am bad," "I am insufficient," "I must not show what I feel," "I do not need anyone," "all men/women/people are the same," "sooner or later they all hurt me," "this person is not who I thought he was."

In such moments the sun that was growing brighter in your chest suddenly dips below the horizon and you experience the curious sensation of "hating," or at least rejecting, the person who dazzled you with love only minutes before. The sensation is that you've been deceived, but there is no deception: rather, every intimate and true relationship brings your most ancient pains to the fore so that they can be healed.

The stronger the commitment in a relationship, the stronger the pain of the perceived "betrayal," and the more spectacular the other's fall from grace in your eyes. The loved one suddenly becomes, in the words of Welwood, "the bad other": a representative of everyone who has hurt, angered or disappointed you in your life. We also build collective "bad others" in our minds, as can be clearly seen in wars, racial confrontations and social conflicts. The more unconscious the response to the anger you feel, the more probable that it will manifest as a desire for revenge and redress ("I'm going to show you that you can't treat me like this!"), which leads to an escalation of aggressions and to the eventual destruction of love.

Here we are again in the waters of the swamp. There is nothing that activates your shadow as quickly and strongly as your relationships with other people. As we discovered previously, the way through this is never to avoid or to go around the swamp, but to wade through it with courage and determination.

What does it mean to go through? To open yourself to the difficult emotions you feel, without judgment or resistance. As we will see in the exercises that follow, the goal is to be able to make room for everything: for the anger you feel, with its multiple layers of memories and past wounds, and also for the love that lies beneath that anger (even though for the moment you can't feel it).

Can every relationship be a route towards integrity and growth? Yes, it can, as long as there is no abuse, maltreatment or violence of any kind, and no serious pathology in either of the people involved. Beyond this proviso, the key is to observe the nature of the connection you have. If you feel a kind of soul resonance with the person, and if you feel that you are seen and deeply understood, this indicates there is a solid foundation on which you both can build.

THE "MAGICAL OTHER" AND DIFFERENTIATION

No relationship, however strong, can heal your wounds without your active involvement. Just as it is easy to fall into the confusion of the "bad other," it can also be tempting to sit back and wait for the arrival of a "magical other"—a term coined by the Jungian analyst James Hollis—meaning a messiah who will rescue you from yourself. "Prince Charming," "better half" and "soulmate" are popular versions of this fantasy. Both the "bad other" and the "magical other" are projections that will take you away from the possibility of forming a true bond. Hollis suggests that we ask ourselves a provocative question: "What am I asking of my partner that I should be doing for myself?" No one, he says, can achieve a better relationship with another person than he has with herself or himself.

In order to meet each other as adults, without tacitly asking the other to save us from ourselves, we must develop an ability that is one of the keys to maturity: *differentiation*.

This ability requires you to balance two vital impulses: *autonomy*, which is the key to following your own impulses and creating your own identity, and *union,* which drives you to join with others and to belong. We are talking here about the same ability that we must acquire as babies if we are to grow and develop into healthy individuals.

In the words of sexologist and psychotherapist David Schnarch, author of *Passionate Marriage: Keeping Love and Intimacy Alive in Committed Relationships*, differentiation is "the ability to maintain your own sense of self when you are emotionally and/or physically close to others—especially as they become increasingly important to you."

Differentiated people can agree without feeling that they are losing their identity and express disagreement without needing to get angry or take emotional distance. That is to say, they can continue being individuals, even in a state of great closeness and intimacy. The opposite of differentiation is emotional fusion. Widely exalted in movies and songs, and in phrases such as: "You make me whole," "Without you I am nothing" or "I will die if you leave me," the desperate intensity of such longing indicates the size of the wound.

Curiously, the more you try to bridge the gap with the other, the more you annihilate the spontaneity and enthusiasm of the relationship. You may fulfill your desire for contact, but at the price of drowning your need for autonomy. You eliminate all uncertainty and, as if by magic, the passion disappears.

There is a physiological component to these processes. Falling in love is an explosive state, powered by neurotransmitters such as dopamine, norepinephrine and phenethylamine (the hormones of attraction and excitement, which are also secreted when you win a prize or consume certain drugs). This hormonal cocktail lasts an average of two years. Left behind in the calmer waters that follow is oxytocin, the hormone of attachment and affection, which invites us to cuddle, pamper each other and come together in mutual comfort.

This never used to be seen as a problem. From the earliest days, marriage was mostly thought of as an instrument to create and sustain a family, and passion was absolutely not a requirement. It was only about two hundred years ago that people began to freely decide what they wanted and expected from their relationships. Until then there was not much possibility of questioning, innovating or choosing how someone wanted to relate to their children, parents, or friends, and what they wanted to give and receive in a romantic relationship.

Freedom brings with it its own dilemmas. Today we ask our partners to fulfill two almost mutually contradictory functions: we want them to be anchors, a source of safety and support; but we also expect them to provide novelty, amazement and excitement.

Sexologist and therapist Esther Perel, author of *Mating in Captivity*, who attracted a global audience with her TED talk "The Secret to Desire in a Long-term Relationship,"* points out that this contradiction has undermined functioning couples who, in their desire for stability, generate such a degree of fusion that they eradicate the space necessary for desire to exist. "The paradox," she says, "is that the very ingredients that nurture love . . . are sometimes the very ingredients that stifle desire."

The cure begins by applying "erotic intelligence." This means accepting that your partner is another person and that the illusion that he belongs to us, or that we know her to perfection, is just that: an illusion. However well you may think you know your partner, you don't know everything: they will always be something of a mystery. As Perel puts it:

> Whereas therapists typically encourage patients to "really get to know" their partners, I often say that "knowing isn't everything." Most couples exchange enough direct talk in the course of daily life. To create more passion, I suggest that they play a bit more with the ambiguity that's inherent to communication. Eroticism can draw its powerful pleasure from fascination with the hidden, the mysterious, and the suggestive.

Here are some exercises to make your relationships into so many paths of growth, self-discovery and connection with life.

EXERCISES TO EXPLORE AND DEEPEN YOUR RELATIONSHIPS

Sustaining a sense of purpose

More than an exercise, this is a meta-exercise: remind yourself every day that your relationships are not a done deal, a finished product; they are not this way or that: they are what you put into them every day. This does not mean that you have to constantly worry about "improving" your relationships. Perfectionism

* www.ted.com/talks/esther_perel_the_secret_to_desire_in_a_long_term_relationship

leads you away from the tender path of vulnerability in which love grows and is nurtured.

Rather, it means that the commitment that you put into getting to know your fellow travelers on the path, and honoring their deep needs (while trying to satisfy your own), will be its own reward. With love and attention, relationships can grow indefinitely in nuance and flavor, just like good wines.

Visualizing your network

The "social atom" is an exercise devised by Jacob Levy Moreno, creator of the experiential form of therapy known as psychodrama, as a way to visualize your current network of relationships in a simple way. It was further expanded by Anne Schützenberger, who suggests incorporating significant objects into the network.

This is how it is done: you take a sheet of paper and place yourself symbolically in the middle (with a cross, a dot or your initials). Then you begin to locate around you the people who are a part of your life, in the following manner:

- the people who are most important to you, or to whom you feel an attachment or are most at ease with, are placed closest to you;
- the people who are the most different from you, or with whom you have problematic relationships, are placed farther away.

You can also include pets, places or objects of significance to you; as well as books, movies and songs. You can make your chart in a single color, or use different hues for each type of relationship. You can also add symbols, drawings and diagrams.

When you have finished, look at your work without judging it and ask yourself how you feel about the patterns that appear. Is your network dense and rich enough? Is it sufficient to sustain you? Is there anything that you feel the need to modify?

Developing intimacy with your emotions

Your emotions are the main vehicle with which you go out to meet the world. Your familiarity with them has a great influence on the quality of your relationships. Robert Augustus Masters proposes an exercise to explore your emotions, and learn to express them with compassion and kindness.

It consists of four steps. You can do these alone, with your partner or with someone else.

1 Identify which emotion(s) you are feeling. Ask yourself: "Do I feel sad? Ashamed? Calm? Happy? Guilty?" Find the answer in your body. If you feel fear, for example, take note of its presence without letting yourself become involved in the stories it evokes. If you feel apathy, be aware that this emotion tends to cover up many others.

2 Say what you are feeling aloud. If you are with your partner or someone else, it is important to limit yourself to naming the emotion, without adding anything to it. "I feel that you don't listen to me" is a perception, not an emotion; "I'm angry" is an emotion.

3 Make sure the other person hears what you are really saying. With an empathetic attitude, ask him to repeat what he has understood and observe whether he has registered the emotion you have expressed in your words. If you are alone, breathe and continue to open yourself to the emotion, without arguing with yourself or criticizing yourself for feeling it.

4 Fill in what you feel with details, without losing contact with the emotion. It is important to prioritize emotional resonance with the other person over any agreement or disagreement about what you have expressed. Ignoring the emotional disconnection that may have occurred makes you more prone to reaction and disagreement. Whenever you feel as if you are getting lost in the details of the story, stop, breathe and reconnect with the emotion. Then express it again in as frank and direct a way as possible.

To summarize the steps of this exercise: identify the emotion, express it, harmonize with the other person and add the necessary details.

Conscious release of emotions

Another exercise suggested by Masters is ideal for those times when you arrive home fizzing with disturbing emotions or thoughts, and you find yourself unloading them on to someone who doesn't deserve it. Either you or your partner can suggest the following method to dissolve the tension.

While the receiver ensures he is consciously present, and while he contains his own feelings, you explain what has happened to make you so upset. The idea is to give free rein to the emotions involved through the voice and the body, and through movement. You can gesticulate in an exaggerated way, shout or dramatize what you feel, kick the floor or punch the air; and you can use whatever language you want. When you have drained all your emotions (for about ten minutes), lie down, relax and wait for your breathing to calm down. Your partner can lie down with you and hold you.

Acknowledging resentment

The only way to deal properly with conflict—and use it to grow—is to go through it but in a conscious way. To do this you need to make room inside yourself for the resentment that conflict provokes. These are the steps that John Welwood recommends:

1 Think about a painful situation involving a friend, relative or partner.
2 Observe how the pain of this situation manifests itself in your body.
3 Pay attention to how it feels to have this person, momentarily, as "an adversary."
4 Ask yourself if this is in any way an old fight. Is there anything familiar about this emotion? How does it manifest today in the conflict with this person?
5 Express your thought about this in the present tense, in a single sentence, as if you are talking to the person. For example: "You don't see me," "You want to take advantage of me," "You treat me badly."
6 Observe if your complaint brings up memories of a familiar feeling.
7 Without judging, observe what it feels like to recognize that an old resentment for not being perfectly loved is still alive in you and affecting your current relationships.

Dissolving resentment

This is another Welwood exercise to transform the pain of the primal wound by offering it your unconditional presence.

1 Think of a way that you don't really feel loved in a current relationship.
2 How does this feeling of an absence of love manifest in your body? Identify the sensations that appear: heaviness, anxiety, stiffness, coldness, emptiness, numbness, discouragement or anything else.
3 Recognize the feeling and sensations in the body and connect them directly to consciousness. Allow your breath to reach and penetrate the feeling of tension.
4 Let the feeling of absence of love persist as it is, without trying to fix it. Make room around the sensations in the body.
5 Open yourself directly to the pain of not feeling loved and allow any resistance to this feeling to fall away. Is it possible to open the heart to this pain, as an experience felt in the body? How do you feel it?
6 Let your awareness penetrate into the center of the pain.

Finding the source of love within us

This is the practice suggested by Welwood.

1 Think of someone who loves you. Feel the love and care of that person.
2 Observe how you associate this pleasant sensation with that person and how you tend to see her as the source of the experience.
3 Stop thinking about the other person and focus on what is happening in your body when you feel loved. Pay special attention to your heart center. Try to recognize the warmth or fullness of the heart as an experience in itself.
4 What does it feel like to be aware of this?

Hugging until relaxed

The sexologist David Schnarch recommends this technique to help couples achieve a kind of intimacy that honors and preserves each person's autonomy. It consists of embracing your partner while holding your own weight, centering yourself and relaxing.

If your partner leans towards you or away, you will not lose your balance because you are standing firmly on your own feet. If necessary, you can take a step back, ground yourself again and resume the hug. It is important that each of you breathe at your own rhythm and that you allow your breathing to become slowly synchronized with your partner's—but without forcing it. Your breathing can fall into and out of step with the other's without you feeling unbalanced because you will not have alienated yourself from your own being in order to feel close.

This exercise reveals the level of differentiation in a couple and at the same time helps to nurture it.

Re-imagining the other

How much do we allow ourselves to wonder about the people with whom we live? To what extent do we tie them to a fixed, immutable image, instead of allowing them to be the changing, dynamic, ultimately unknowable beings that they are? James Hillman says: "Love alone is not enough. Without imagination, love stales into sentiment, duty, boredom. Relationships fail not because we have stopped loving but because we first stopped imagining."

It's not about pretending that another person is different to who she is, but about recognizing the stranger who actually lives in that person and letting your imagination soar to the eternally mysterious places that dwell in every being.

Practicing kindness

It may sound like Grandmother's advice or a platitude, but it has to be said:
nothing nourishes a relationship as much as the care and attention that you
give to the other person each day. What counts far more than big gestures,
gifts, declarations of love, and all such spectacular stuff, are small daily acts of
kindness: listening with interest to what the other needs to tell you; answering
a question in a considerate way even when you are tired, anxious or busy with
something else. We could cite numerous studies to corroborate this truth: the
occurrence or not of acts of kindness in a relationship can predict with a high
degree of accuracy which couples will still be together five years from now. But
let's give credit to Grandmother, who knew this without having to refer to a
scientific study: if you want to be in a loving relationship, treat your partner
with love.

And so we come to the best kept secret in the village, the one preserved in
the most secure chest stored in the most hidden attic of the most out-of-
sight castle in the world: you can only reach the highest level of love if
you are willing to love the other person for their differences. To discover
similarities with someone else is a delightful experience; but to learn to
converse with another and their peculiar mix of sensitivities and fears,
preferences and aversions, gifts and limitations, wisdom and madness, is
the key that opens the chest of spiritual gold.

We spend much of our lives longing to achieve perfect relationships—
with our partners, our parents, our children, our friends. Eventually we
learn that the only possible way that we can fit with another person is to
make every effort to file down our own sharp edges, and attend to every
aspect of our personality that gets in the way of truly meeting them. The
myriad ways we fit together is never static and perfect, like a finished
puzzle; it is beautiful and dynamic, like life.

Stage 7

THE FIRE
Reclaim Your Rites

Many years ago, there was a village where lived a rabbi. Every time the village went through a time of difficulty, the members of the community followed the rabbi to a certain part of the forest and they all stood around a certain tree, chanted certain prayers and performed certain gestures. That was enough.

Years passed; the rabbi died. There was a famine. The elders of the village went to the forest and searched for the sacred tree.

They did not remember the gestures, but they chanted the prayers. That was enough.

More years passed. People left the village; new people arrived; traditions were lost. One day there was a drought. There were no more elders in the village to know what to do. The young people did not remember the ceremony. They only knew that in difficult times their elders had gone into the forest to sing and to make sacred gestures. They searched for a tree; they sang the little they remembered; they made the gestures that occurred to them.

And that was enough.

Old Hasidic Tale

It's a dark night. The beating of drums reverberates through the earth and a polyphony of voices sounds in the undergrowth. Squatting around the campfire, the men mark the rhythm. The women sing and dance; turning in circles, they move around the fire in imitation of the movement of the sun. Their voices and their bodies give thanks for the harvest and the goodwill of heaven. With the first rays of the sun, the ceremony comes to an end. Gratitude has been offered; the ritual has been performed. It is done.

The baby curls up in the arms of her great-grandmother, in the living room of a modern suburban house. Several generations of women in the family—from ten to ninety years old—form a circle around them. They express wishes for the little one; gifts are offered; toasts are made; songs are sung. When the moment arrives, the great-grandmother draws a symbol with fragrant oil on the little girl's forehead and whispers a blessing. Suddenly she begins to speak in Russian, her native tongue, surprising everyone, perhaps herself most of all. The ceremony concludes with an outpouring of blessings for the newborn. Each one endorsed with a vigorous "So may it be!", intoned by the chorus of female voices. The girl has been named, she is one of the family. It is done.

Many things have changed in our technocratic and secularized society but, mysteriously, rites and ceremonies have not lost their place. Today, as yesterday, these simple or elaborate symbolic acts transform newborns into community members, children into adolescents, adolescents into adults. They make princes into kings, medical students into doctors, ordinary citizens into presidents. With rituals we bind couples together; we bid farewell to our loved ones; we greet new cycles; we turn profane places into sacred spaces; houses and buildings into homes.

WHAT IS A RITE AND WHY DOES ITS POWER ENDURE?

A rite is the staging of a psycho-spiritual reality using the power of symbol. What is a symbol? It is an image, object, letter or figure that represents something other than itself, often something of an immaterial nature. Unlike a sign, which has one meaning (a red traffic light means "stop"), a symbol can have multiple meanings (in the West, a dragon is synonymous with danger; in China, it indicates prosperity and good fortune).

Rites use symbols because symbols are the language of the soul and the unconscious. When a bride and groom exchange rings in the marriage ceremony, the act is imbued with layers of meaning: the circularity of the ring evokes eternity and completeness; the gold speaks of the power of the sun; the ring finger of the left hand of the betrothed indicates a connection to the heart.

No one needs a detailed explanation of all these symbolic layers: everyone who witnesses the gesture of ring-giving understands it as a promise of love and commitment.

The German archaeologist Walter Andrae says in his book *Die ionische Säule: Bauform oder Symbol?* (*The Ionic Column: Design or Symbol?*):

> Anyone who is surprised that a formal symbol can not only remain alive for millennia, but also return to life after an interruption of thousands of years, should remember that the power of the spiritual world—of which the symbol is a part—is eternal.

The Functions of a Rite

A rite fulfills certain functions, including the following:

- Creates or strengthens bonds between people.
- Serves as reassurance and stability during a crisis.
- Links the past with the present and recalls the elements of the founding myth.
- Separates *kairos* (time of the soul) from *chronos* (calendar time).
- Helps heal body and soul.
- Recognizes and honors changes (rites of passage, of age, stage, cycles), while at the same time keeping participants connected to what is deep and unchanging.
- Consecrates new statuses, roles and skills.
- Helps say goodbye.
- Offers a form of adult play, with a serious purpose.
- Honors the sacred at the heart of everyday life.

In all these ways, ritual acts, large or small, simple or spectacular, make the invisible world visible. Every time we stop to mark a significant passage or to celebrate an event, we pay tribute to the spiritual reality that underlies the material world.

"Ceremonies are the way we remember to remember," says Robin Wall Kimmerer, the biologist who tells the story of the Potawatomi people in "The Jungle." What are we remembering? At a personal level, the events that mark our lives and give them meaning. As families, the facts that constitute the identity of the clan. As societies, we remember the milestones that created the bonds that hold us together.

While rites and ceremonies (the latter are generally more formal and elaborate affairs) have traditionally been associated with religion, their roots are older and vaster. Rites have always been multimedia events: they integrated storytelling, singing, dancing and acting; and they provided the matrix from which art, medicine, education and sports would emerge.

Still today our lives are filled from end to end with secular ceremonies: birthday parties, anniversaries, baby blessings, graduation ceremonies, housewarmings, ship launchings, national holidays and seasonal festivities. We also indulge in daily rites of etiquette and good manners such as handshakes, applause, greetings and expressions including "cheers!", "sorry" and "thank you."

Tom Driver, author of *Liberating Rites: Understanding the Transforming Power of Ritual*, defines human beings as "ceremonial animals." But we are not the only ones: other species have also evolved ritual gestures to communicate symbolically: the dances of bees; the mating displays of peacocks; and the pounding of chests by gorillas.

The difference is that in human beings rites are also expressions of myths (those stories that tell us about who we are). This is how the great Joseph Campbell puts it:

A ritual is the enactment of a myth. And, by participating in the ritual, you are participating in the myth. And since myth is a projection of the depth wisdom of the psyche, by participating in a ritual, participating in the myth, you are being, as it were, put in accord with that wisdom, which is the wisdom that is inherent within you anyhow. Your consciousness is being re-minded of the wisdom of your own life. I think ritual is terribly important.

If one of the functions of myth is to provide a narrative that helps people make the transition to a new stage of life, the rite involved is the sequence of actions that inscribes this narrative in the body and in consciousness (and, at the same time, consciousness is the primary driver of rites). An act that is repeated automatically and without consciousness—like brushing your teeth—is not a rite, but a routine.

In his iconic 1908 work *The Rites of Passage*, ethnographer Arnold van Gennep described three key moments in rites or ceremonies: separation; the liminal experience (from *limen*, which in Latin means "threshold") or transformation; and return or reincorporation.

Let's look at an example.

Three moments in a marriage ceremony

Separation. The moment in which the bride and groom walk down the aisle to the altar. They are soon to leave behind their old identities (as single people), but have not yet acquired their new ones as a married couple. The rite serves as protection during that period of depersonalization that is part of every transition.

The ritual act itself (or transformation). This is the focus of the event and carries the energy of the participants to a crescendo. In the marriage ceremony it is the moment in which the priest or presiding official tells the couple what their obligations will be, receives their vows and declares them "husband and wife."

Incorporation. The newlyweds turn towards the community (the congregation) and return together into it, carrying with them their new identity.

Not every rite follows this structure strictly, but there will always be a defined beginning, development and closure; stages that set the act apart from calendar time and mark it as a special event.

In native cultures adolescent rites of passage were especially important, as they initiated young people into the roles that the community needed them to fulfill. These rites for boys were arduous and sometimes violent because they needed to clearly mark the difference between infancy and adulthood, and beget warriors for the tribe. Girls, on the other hand, had a clear bodily sign of the change—the onset of menstruation—to remind them that they were now women, and could no longer behave like children.

Today, there are no universally accepted rites of passage. As a consequence, adolescence is extended or even becomes a permanent fixture in the psyche of the young. In an attempt to compensate for this absence of ritual, adolescents sometimes create their own ceremonies. But these ceremonies do not have adults in charge, directing them and receiving initiates into the heart of the community. Sometimes they take on dark twists, as is the case in criminal gangs, where acceptance into the group is earned through an act of violence.

It is important to note that a rite is in itself morally neutral. Its worth depends on the intention that guides it and on the awareness with which it is observed. There are rites that are ineffectual (they fail to fulfill the function intended) and there are rites that perpetuate oppression, such as female genital mutilation. It is as necessary to criticize violent or dysfunctional rites as it is to praise wholesome ones.

These days there is a growing movement to recover or create rites of passage for adolescents, under the direction of adults. Young people are taken to remote wild places and taught survival skills such as learning to make a fire, build a shelter and live on wild plants. These and other such experiences are beginning to reconstruct the path of initiation that for millennia helped individuals grow into adulthood.

It is a path that tests courage, but also offers support, encouragement and guidance. Joseph Campbell sums it up in a story he was fond of telling: "A bit of advice given to a young Native American at the time of his initiation: as you go the way of life, you will see a great chasm. Jump. It is not as wide as you think."

Ritual Creativity

If rites require first of all *the stopping of time*, can we find a place for them in our increasingly virtual, technological and accelerated lives? Can we give up those rites that have lost their validity? Can we, in turn, create new rites, more in line with the reality that we live? The answer to all three questions is: yes!

Formerly, it was thought that rites were acts that societies performed exclusively to preserve their institutions. While this conservative function still exists, today we know that they can also serve the opposite purpose. Ronald Grimes, a Canadian professor of ritual studies and author of *Deeply Into the Bone: Re-inventing Rites of Passage*, explained this to me in conversation: "That began to change in North America in the 1960s with civil rights, feminism and the anti-war movement. During all of these ritual was taken and reinvented on the streets and in the bedroom. No longer a captive of in-power governments or established churches, such rituals became more improvisational and more socially critical."

New developments in society brought the possibility of creating new rites; modifying existing ones; or even improvising completely, following the inspiration of the moment, as happens in those three close relatives of ritual – music, dance and the theater. In such cases people sometimes reach for elements from other traditions, which they adapt to their purposes. A wide range of ritual gestures and ceremonies has become popular and transcended their cultural boundaries.

A case in point is the celebration of the Fiesta de la Pachamama, which takes place on August 1st amongst descendants of the Incas, in South America. It is a typical festivity of the north-west of Argentina, and is of Aymara origin. It is also held in Bolivia and in Peru. On this day houses, businesses and people are perfumed with an herb called *muña muña*, as well as myrrh and sandalwood. Food and drink offerings are made to *Pachamama* (Mother Earth), asking her for a good harvest and protection. Participants also drink a liquor flavored with rue and offer a splash of it to the earth. This last gesture has been adopted in cities and the offering can be made using any available soil, even a pot on the balcony.

In addition, on June 24th, some urban communities celebrate the Inti Raymi, or resurrection of the sun, another Andean rite that marks the new year and the southern hemisphere's winter solstice. Around the same dates (June 21 to 24) others honor the We Tripantu, the celebration of the Mapuche New Year, with stories and songs around a bonfire.

Some people incorporate loose elements of these and other festivities into their own ceremonies. Is it legitimate to borrow rites from other cultures? Grimes answers: "For as long as we have an archaeological or historical record it is clear that people have borrowed, traded, bought and stolen rituals. In this respect, rituals are a bit like music or stories. Sometimes people are territorial about them, and the result is copyright or some other form of control. At other times, people freely exchange rituals or ritual knowledge. So the only way to answer the question is situational, by asking: 'Who cares? Who might be offended? Who would not?' This is the ethical dimension of the problem. Then there is the practical dimension: How long does it take you to embody, or digest, a borrowed ritual element? How do you overcome stilted or self-conscious ritualizing? How long does it take to 'break in' a new ritual element, to become adept at it?"

The truth is that conducting our own rites is a way of reappropriating the direct experience of spirituality. In order to do this, it is useful to know the most common constituents of rites and ceremonies.

Elements That Compose a Rite

The intention. This is the most important part of the rite. A ceremony can be very elaborate, but if it is carried out automatically it won't have any power. By contrast, the simplest act can be powerful if the intention behind it is strong. In group rites the intention of the leader can inspire and boost the energy of all those present. In addition, it is important to remember that a rite is morally neutral. If it is undertaken with negative intentions, it is debased. A rite elevates and transforms participants only if it is driven by love.

The invocation. In a formal ceremony it is common to begin with an invocation. If those gathered believe in a particular deity they may dedicate the rite to it, or ask for its support in performing the rite. It is also possible to invoke "the forces of the universe," one's own "higher self," the power of love, or of life itself. Several native communities of North America call to "the four directions" (east, south, west, north) before beginning their rites, to ask for their blessing.

The altar. The concept of an altar is traditionally associated with religious ceremonies. But the truth is that we set up altars without even realizing it: you may place photos on a shelf in the very center of a room; or arrange flowers, stones or ornaments in a certain configuration in your workplace. What these objects indicate is that the place, or what those objects represent, has significance for you and you want to honor them. The altar is the focal point of a ceremony: it summons the energies of the participants and reminds them of what brings them together. If the people are arranged in a circle, the altar can be placed in the center, on a cloth chosen for this purpose. Or it can be at the front, next to the person presiding over the rite. More important than the location of the altar is that the symbols it holds are meaningful to the participants. Typically, some representation of the sacred is combined with elements linked specifically to the rite that is to be performed. One thing that is not usually missing is fire: nothing says "the rite has begun" like lighting a candle.

Elements of nature. Perhaps because they remind us of ancestral rites, or because our souls recognize that nature is our true home, rites gain strength when we incorporate some natural elements into them. Even outside of specific rites, it is possible to assemble a "seasonal altar" in your house, in which elements of each season—flowers, leaves, pine cones, seeds—are showcased throughout the year. Its preparation and renewal becomes a rite in itself.

The four elements. Today, we know that the world is made of more than four elements, but in our imagination earth, air, fire and water still have great symbolic weight. You can include them by using a feather to represent the air; a bowl full of seashells for water; a candle or smudge stick, for fire; some stones or a tree branch, for earth. The elements can also be a central part of the rite. For example, you can write down something you want to let go of on a piece of paper, and throw that paper into a stream or river; plant a seed with the intention of something new growing in your life; make a bonfire to celebrate the arrival of winter; or burn sage (or another herb if you prefer) throughout your house to dispel stagnant energies, and consciously breathe in its scent to calm your thoughts and renew your spirit.

The body. Although the meaning of the rite is rooted in the invisible plane, the strength of the ceremony rests on performing bodily actions. Any physical gesture, no matter how small, strengthens the act. A good ritual activates the wisdom of the body and mobilizes the emotions. In India, a ceremonial country by nature, it is common to employ mudras: hand gestures that summon a certain kind of energy or psychic state. Prayers from different traditions naturally involve specific actions or postures that help predispose the soul to sacred communion.

Rhythm. Rhythm is present in our lives from the womb, and it affects us deeply throughout our lives. According to Michael Harner, synthesizer of core shamanic practices, the most common way of entering into a ritual trance (or "shamanic state of consciousness") is through the beat of a drum. Neurological studies have shown that after hearing or playing a drum for twelve minutes, struck at a rate of four to seven beats per second, our brain waves attune to the instrument and enter a theta rhythm. The state of expanded awareness that this rhythm produces resembles the one fostered by meditation. "Science can't explain the efficacy of rituals," says German psychotherapist Ruediger Dahlke. However, we do know that in a ritual trance the right and left side of the brain may harmonize in a state that facilitates transformation.

Singing and dancing. These too have deep roots in ritual. In some shamanic cultures singing alone was considered powerful enough to heal a person, attaining what in that worldview was known as "soul recovery." Song and dance are often essential elements of celebrations, but they also have their place in the funerary rites of diverse cultures.

Closure. It is customary to finish a rite by bidding farewell to the forces summoned at the beginning, putting out the ritual fire and singing a few words or reciting a poem or prayer. A closing expression that transcends religions is "May it be so!" To further strengthen the intention, the closing words may be even more emphatic: "It is so!"

Kinds of Rites

Family rites

Family life is full of rites. In the absence of positive and significant rituals, a kind of rigid and empty *ritualizing* behavior may appear. Thus, good rites can be a form of preventive medicine. Children appreciate true rites because they speak to their authentic and profound identities. Some occasions when rites may be observed are: during mealtimes; before going to bed; at the beginning or ending of classes at school; when a child loses a tooth; on the occasion of academic or professional achievements; cultural, religious or physical initiations (such as menarche, for girls); the death of a loved one; and transitions, such as going off to college, or moving house.

In *Rituals in Families and Family Therapy*, Evan Imber-Black, Janine Roberts and Richard Whiting explore the importance of rituals in the clinical treatment of families. Therapists, they explain, have discovered that decisive changes are set in motion when a family with difficulties undertakes carefully designed rituals, such as those pertaining to identity, belonging and celebrations.

Rites with friends

Now, people ask me, what rituals can we have today? My answer is, what are you doing? What is important in your life? What is important, they say, is having dinner with their friends. *That* is a ritual.

Joseph Campbell integrates ritual in everyday life here. Rites are more or less effective, more or less satisfactory, in proportion to the care and conscious intention that we put into them. Rituals can arise among friends spontaneously, but we can also deepen their efficacy by paying special attention:

- Could we cook a meal together some time instead of going out to eat?
- Could we choose a dish with special meaning for one of our group?
- Could we propose a toast in honor of some important event for the group?
- What occasions could we celebrate or give thanks for beyond birthdays and anniversaries?

Rites of blessing

To bless means to wish good for another person by gesture or word. For a long time, blessing was thought to be the privilege of religious officiants. But the truth is that we can all bless, and we all do. The mother who kisses her daughter's forehead before she goes out is an example of this very human disposition to accompany and protect those we love. What can we bless? The birth of children; new houses; launching a project; crossing a threshold of some kind. Most of all, we can bless each other. There are infinite ways to bless through words and gestures and it's important to allow yourself to find your own. We can also be inspired by tradition and place our hands, lovingly and consciously, on the person we wish to bless, and anoint him with our intention as we speak a few words from the heart. Where love is the motor, mistakes are rare, and usually forgivable.

Rites in solitude

Although rites are more usually communal events, they can be just as effective on your own. In fact, sometimes just to give yourself a moment of solitude is an important rite in itself. Campbell again:

> You must have a room, or a certain hour or so a day, where you don't know what was in the newspapers that morning, you don't know who your friends are, you don't know what you owe anybody, you don't know what anybody owes to you. This is a place where you can simply experience and bring forth what you are and what you might be. This is the place of creative incubation. At first you may find that nothing happens there. But if you have a sacred place and use it, something eventually will happen.

Rites of transformation

Rites were formerly thought of as acts to preserve order and stability in a community, but in fact they can also help nurture new realities into being. For example, rites can forge or strengthen bonds in blended families; they can help make an adopted child feel that he belongs; and they can help family members accept their new life after a separation.

Rites of farewell

Saying goodbye to our loved ones has always been one of the most heart wrenching experiences we can face. We use rites in order to not grieve alone, and to ground ourselves in a mythical narrative that can help us accept the inexplicable. But these pre-established rites do not always represent us, or reflect our view of the world; nor do they necessarily honor the unique connection that we had with the person we lost. It is time to re-appropriate this vital rite of passage. What can you do when your heart is broken and you can't even deal with the most elementary aspects of life? You can choose simple words to express your grief, your gratitude, your respect towards the person who has passed. You don't need to be a poet. As the great Mary Oliver puts it in her poem *Thirst:* "Just/pay attention, then patch/a few words together and don't try/to make them elaborate, this isn't/a contest. . ."

If your voice breaks, a gesture is enough: take a bow, bring your hands together over your heart, share a few moments of silence, let out a liberating round of applause. Your soul knows what it needs to do; all you have to do is listen.

The poet Oriah Mountain Dreamer says, "Every act I live while I am fully awake cannot help but be both prayer and lovemaking." Ritualizing life often and passionately is the equivalent of living with your eyes and heart wide open; of honoring the mystery of existence every step of the way.

The naturalist and poet Diane Ackerman (who we met in "The Garden") vows to do just that in her inspired poem "School prayer," which concludes:

> In the name of the sun and its mirrors
> and the day that embraces it
> and the cloud veils drawn over it
> and the uttermost night
> and the male and the female
> and the plants bursting with seed
> and the crowning seasons
> of the firefly and the apple,
> I will honor all life
> —wherever and in whatever form
> it may dwell—on Earth my home,
> and in the mansions of the stars.

May it be so! It is so.

THE LIGHTHOUSE
Focus Your Mind

Calm the waters of your mind and the universe and the stars
will be reflected in your soul.
Rumi

The bad news is you're falling through the air and there's nothing to
hold on to, no parachutes. The good news is there's no ground.
Chögyam Trungpa

The wind swirls the sand around and shakes the palm fronds along the coast. The trees, calm a moment ago, look like enraged monsters in the sudden storm. The darkness and the frenzied motion cause us to lose all sense of direction. Suddenly, a beam of light sweeps across the beach. In its triangle of illumination everything returns to its place: the trees are once again trees, the coast is the coast, the sea is the sea. This is the power of the lighthouse: it cuts through the dark, reminding us that our true home is within us, and always within reach. In the words of the Indian sage Ajahn Chah: "If you are lost in the forest, you are not really lost. You are lost only when you forget who you are."

This powerful beacon is our consciousness, that mysterious faculty that underlies all phenomena of mind, and that possesses the crucial attribute of self-awareness. We all get glimpses of this intelligence sometimes. It shows up when a painful event blindsides you and you are jolted awake from the state of apathy or drowsiness that we are all prone to falling into. In such a moment you become suddenly and keenly aware of what really matters. The same experience can be triggered by some gesture made by a loved one; by an emotionally moving scene; or when the simple joy of being alive overwhelms you and for a moment everything seems to shine from within. In these moments, the question of meaning . . . loses all meaning.

We don't live in such a state most of the time. The world is noisy; the mind is noisier still; and it is easy to lose contact with the clarity of the lighthouse. This is why human beings have over millennia created and perfected contemplative practices: as a way to help clear the mists and bring back the light. One of the oldest and most universal of these practices is meditation.

How long have we been meditating? Although some archaeologists trace its beginnings to 5,000 years BC, the first written records appear in the Hindu tradition of the Vedanta around 1500 BC and, a little later, in Taoist China and Buddhist India. There are also variations from the beginnings of Christianity, Judaism and Islam, among other traditions. A historical explanation is that meditation may have traveled the Silk Road, being adapted and transformed as it moved from culture to culture.

In the twentieth century it arrived in the West through the counter-cultural revolution of the 1960s. The flower power and anti-war generations found inspiration and encouragement in Eastern religions. They adopted yoga and transcendental meditation, while the Beatles and other icons of the time became (albeit briefly) dazzled by the teachings of the Maharishi Mahesh Yogi and other gurus.

Years later, physician Jon Kabat-Zinn created a version of meditation stripped of all cultural and religious elements and presented it to the University of Massachusetts, under the name "Mindfulness-Based Stress Reduction Program" (MBSR). With science behind it, mindfulness and meditation would go on to take the world by storm. Here are a few of the scientifically validated benefits of these time-honored practices:

- A decrease in the activity of the amygdala (which is linked to alertness and to the production of the stress hormone, cortisol).
- Increased activity of the prefrontal cortex, which facilitates thinking.
- Improved focus and memory.
- Increased immunity.
- Lowered blood pressure.
- Promotion of restful sleep.
- 50-percent reduction in the recurrence of depression.

Health benefits aside, people eventually began to cultivate this practice for less utilitarian reasons, finally coming to understand why gurus, yogis and masters of all traditions had been promoting meditation long before anyone ever pronounced the word "cortisol." The guardians of these traditions did not take physiological measurements, but they observed that those who committed themselves to this discipline managed to live with greater calm, wisdom and generosity, becoming more available to themselves and to others.

What possible relation could there be between these lofty virtues and the act of sitting, eyes closed and legs crossed, in order to simply breathe? Let's take a look at meditation from the start.

WHAT IS MEDITATION?

One possible answer is: meditation is replacing discursive thinking with an alternative object of attention; in other words, focusing your mind. Buddhists have a great name for the discursive mind: they call it the "monkey mind," because of its tendency to pass from one thought to another, like a monkey jumping non-stop from branch to branch. Here is how it sounds: "I'm going to sit down and write now, but first I'd better jot down what I have to do today, because if I don't I'll forget to make an appointment with the dentist, and to buy milk and butter and oh! Today is Sandra's birthday! I wonder if she'll like the book I bought her? What if she already has it? I better not write a dedication in it, just in case she needs to change it. Maybe I'll just make myself a cup of coffee and write her a card. Coffee? There's no coffee! Boy, it's going to be hot today. It's already getting warm and it's only nine a.m . . . nine a.m. already, and I haven't even started to write!"

It's not that there's anything wrong with the mind thinking. Thinking is its task; we don't want it to stop. But its tendency to digress creates a level of mental noise that can become deafening. Freed to do its own thing, the mind pulls us back and forth like a tide fluctuating between the past and the future, and rarely stops at the only place where we can really find peace: the present.

Why do we meditate? We meditate to achieve a goal that appears simple: to bring the mind to meet the body where it lives, which is always, inexorably, the present moment. When the mind and body are in the same place, we are available for whatever we are feeling, thinking or perceiving. This is not always pleasant, of course. We gladly attend to enjoyable emotions such as love, joy or amazement, but it is much more of a challenge to be awake and present for pain, fear, anguish or loneliness. And why should we? Not as a form of masochism, certainly, but as a way to receive these experiences fully in our awareness, and help them heal. We know that suppressing or repressing disagreeable emotions does not diminish their impact. Rather, it makes them worse in the long run, since repressed emotions turn up as anxiety, or as a variety of physical symptoms. On the other hand, receiving these emotions with an open heart allows them to release their grip on us and dissolve. As the analogy goes, a spoonful of salt in a glass of water renders the water undrinkable, but the same spoonful of salt in a lake becomes imperceptible. Consciousness has the capacity to become that wide and placid lake, in which everything can be received and transformed.

How does it accomplish this feat? By ceasing to resist life as it is, moment to moment, especially when things don't go our way. This was the great discovery of Gautama Buddha (on whose teachings Buddhism is based) when he reached enlightenment under the Bodhi tree in the fifth century BC. "I have seen all there is to see and know all there is to know in order to be able to free myself completely from all illusion and all suffering," he declared. And this is the path he proposed: to face all that life brings us without attachment or aversion, but with courage, equanimity and clear-eyed acceptance.

Taking the One Seat

Jack Kornfield is a much loved contemporary Buddhist author and teacher who is known for the honesty of his teachings, which do not hide or diminish the challenges of the spiritual path. In *A Path With Heart: A Guide Through the Dangers and Promises of the Spiritual Life*, Kornfield says, "When we take the one seat on our meditation cushion we become our own monastery. We create the compassionate space that allows for the arising of all things: sorrows, loneliness, shame, desire, regret, frustration, happiness."

Spiritual transformation is a profound process that requires discipline in order to see and release mental habits that divert you from your purpose, and meditation is a superb tool to help build that discipline. This was the advice of Ajahn Chah, who we have heard from already, who was a teacher of Kornfield and many others:

> Just go into the room and put one chair in the center. Take the seat in the center of the room, open the doors and the windows, and see who comes to visit. You will witness all kinds of scenes and actors, all kinds of temptations and stories, everything imaginable. Your only job is to stay in your seat. You will see it all arise and pass, and out of this, wisdom and understanding will come.

In *A Path With Heart*, Kornfield tells the story of a man who attended one of his meditation retreats. The man had lost his young daughter in a car accident. He had been driving the car when it happened, so his grief was shot through with an overwhelming sense of guilt. When he arrived at the retreat he had already gone through many seminars, had been blessed by a great swami and had taken vows with a nun from southern India. He made his meditation cushion at the retreat look like a nest: all around it were crystals, feathers, rosary beads and pictures of great gurus. Each time he sat down he prayed to all these gurus and sang and recited a dozen sacred mantras. He did all this in order to heal himself, he said. But perhaps it was also a way of keeping his grief at a prudent distance. Kornfield recalls:

> After a few days I asked him if he would be willing to simply sit down, without all his sacred objects, without prayers or songs or any other practice. The next time he went to meditate, he just sat down. Within five minutes he was crying. He had finally allowed himself to take a seat in the midst of his pain, and had finally begun to mourn. We all exercise this kind of courage when we take the one seat.

HOW TO MEDITATE

There are as many ways of meditating as there are schools, teachers and traditions, but they all focus on training the mind to help it find a foothold in the present, which is the space of being. As a starting point, we will explore a meditation technique from the ancient Indian tradition of Vipassana (which means "to see things as they are" in Sanskrit). Since it is the modality that Buddha practiced to reach enlightenment, it does not seem like a bad place to begin.

1 Find a stable and comfortable posture in which you can remain attentive and conscious of your body. You can sit on a cushion with your legs crossed, or in a chair with your feet resting on the floor. The important thing is to find a posture that allows you to remain still for several minutes. Your back should be upright but without rigidity or discomfort.
2 Imagine that your body from the waist down is rooted in the earth and is heavy and stable. From the waist up, unfold yourself in the direction of the sky, without tension but aspiring to height (as if the top of your head was hanging by a golden thread from a cloud). Keep your chin parallel to the floor.
3 If you choose to sit on the floor you can use a thick cushion, so that your pelvis is slightly higher than the knees and the knees can rest comfortably on the floor.
4 Rest your hands on your lap or on your knees, allowing your shoulders to relax, your chest to open and your belly to loosen.

5 Let your eyes close gently. If you feel you are going to fall asleep, you can keep them half-open, resting your gaze gently on a point on the ground about a meter away.

6 Begin to pay attention to the sounds you can hear: listen for soft and loud sounds; sounds near and far and in the middle distance; continuous sounds and those that are abrupt.

7 Then observe any physical sensations: the feel of the fabric of your clothes against your skin; the temperature and humidity of the air; the posture of your body.

8 Next direct your attention to the activity of your mind: thoughts, emotions, expectations; any memories that may be present.

9 Finally, take notice of your breathing, using it as an anchor for your attention. You can focus on your nostrils if you want: observe how they move with each inhalation and exhalation; how the air has a different temperature when you breathe in to when you breathe out. Or you can focus on your belly, noticing how it inflates and deflates like a balloon with each breath. A third way to be aware of your breathing is to pay attention to the rhythmic ascent and descent of your diaphragm. Whichever focal point you choose, notice how no breath is the same as the next; examine each one with curiosity. Feel yourself breathing.

10 Every time a thought appears, notice it as if you were watching a cloud pass across the sky, without getting attached to it. Or you can imagine that you are standing barefoot in a running stream in which your thoughts and sensations are like leaves that are carried by the current; they huddle for a few moments around your ankles and then go on their way. You do nothing to stop them. Soon enough, you will realize that neither your thoughts nor your emotions have the solid quality you may ascribe to them. In the same way, see if you can begin to see the world as it truly is: impermanent, fluid, dynamic and in a constant state of renewal.

11 If you realize that you have "gotten hooked" by a thought, simply bring your attention gently back to your breath. Attention needs to be trained like a restless puppy: with patience and kindness.

12 Start by practicing this technique for 5 minutes, and extend it as and when you feel ready, until you reach 20 minutes. Then, aim to meditate once in the morning (preferably before breakfast) and again in the afternoon or evening, if possible immediately before going to sleep. It is more useful to meditate for a few minutes each day, anchoring the practice firmly into your routine, than to go all out and sit for one hour, but only once a week.

Labeling

Another meditative practice to try is to label what you perceive. Begin, as always, by paying attention to your breathing. Every time you catch yourself thinking, silently say to yourself: "thought." If you want to be more specific you can label the thought "worry," "anticipation," "memory" or any other pertinent label. If you perceive an emotion, call it by its name: "boredom," "anxiety," "sadness." After naming it, continue to watch closely, because another emotion is likely to be revealed underneath it. For example: "loneliness." It is easy to fall into the temptation of thinking that you can only truly begin to meditate when all those annoying thoughts or emotions finally subside.

The truth is that to meditate is to live peacefully with all these stimuli. In her book *True Love*, meditation teacher Sharon Salzberg tells a charming and revealing anecdote. She was once sitting in a monastery in India, receiving a Dharma teaching (a Buddhist lesson) about equanimity, which is the sense of balance born of our capacity to detach ourselves from our passions and aversions. She was young and enthusiastic, and she loved what she was hearing. It seemed to be the answer to all her problems, the exact wisdom she needed for her life. Just one thought kept her from enjoying the talk fully: if only she could get rid of the pain in her knees caused by sitting down to meditate, she would really be able to take in the teaching. It didn't take her long to see the irony of her situation: she was yearning for the perfect conditions in order to be able to enjoy a talk about not yearning for the perfect conditions for anything.

Buddhists speak of the yearning mind, referring to the egoistic mind's tendency to want to control reality to suit its predilections and always want things to be other than as they are. In his lovely book *Meditation for Beginners*, Kornfield shares his own struggles with this conundrum:

> You are sitting there, heeding the breath when suddenly your mind says, "if only I had something to eat," "if it was only a little warmer," "if it was only a little cooler" or "if I only had a more comfortable meditation cushion." The problem with the yearning mind is that no matter how much it gets what it wants, it never stops.

So what can we do? When desires emerge, you can label them: "desire, desire, desire," or you can think "lack, lack, lack, lack." And you can explore the feeling with curiosity. If you are hungry, where do you feel the hunger? In your stomach? In your mouth? In your heart? Often, the desire to eat hides hunger of an emotional nature. When you calmly observe what is happening, you learn to recognize the ephemeral nature of desire, and realize that the fact of feeling an impulse does not force you to blindly obey it.

In the same way, if sitting down to meditate causes you to become terribly drowsy, it may simply mean that you were tired and had not noticed it. Or it may indicate that your body is not yet accustomed to remaining calm and alert. If this is the case, take some deep breaths and name this state, in the same way as before—"Sleepiness, sleepiness, sleepiness"—and see if the state transforms or drains away by itself.

If the predominant emotion you feel is "restlessness" you can also investigate how it feels in the body, while naming it. The worst-case scenario, says Kornfield humorously, is to confront the feeling and say to yourself, "Okay, this will kill me. I'm going to become the first meditator in history to die of restlessness." Ultimately, what makes these states so difficult is not the emotions or sensations themselves, but the resistance we put up against feeling them. Once you make room for them, they lose much of their power.

Witness Consciousness

Put down this book for a moment, and ask yourself a question: "Who is reading?" Or, perhaps: "Who is listening to the words I read?"

The question might befuddle you at first, but soon you will realize that, while the mind is busy churning out thoughts, memories, plans, fantasies and emotions, or reading the words on this page, there is at all times a silent witness that is observing all this activity. We can call this aspect of ourselves the "witness consciousness." It is that quiet and peaceful space from which thoughts arise, and into which they dissolve. We can liken it to the sky that is the backdrop for the moving clouds; the canvas on which the painter places his brushstrokes; the screen on which a movie is projected. To find it, try this very simple exercise: Say the word "hello" in your mind. Say it louder. Now scream it. Who hears the "hello"? What was there before you said it, and what is left when the word has gone? This ever-present, all-pervading witness consciousness is the portal to peace.

The ancient traditions have always known this, and continue to teach it to this day. In his ashram in India, the sage Ajahn Chah was known for catching aspiring monks in moments of anger, doubt or irritation, and asking them (not provokingly but with a smile on his face), "Who is irritated? Who is angry?" Then he would ask them, "Can you rest in the consciousness that perceives these states?"

We can learn to rest in the pure consciousness that knows, the consciousness that remains immutable in the midst of the most difficult thoughts and emotions. How? Here is one way.

Conscious breathing

Just observing your breath can help you enter into a meditative state. Even better than observing it is feeling it: paying attention to how each breath feels, at each moment. No two breaths are the same, so this exploration can help you to stay connected to the steady flow of life.

However, sometimes the mind is so restless that you may find it hard to sit still long enough to watch your breathing. In this case you can try some specific breathing practices to help you find stillness. Here are some possibilities:

BREATHING PRACTICES

Breathing practice for beginners

- Inhale deeply through your nose to the count of three; hold your breath to the count of two; then exhale slowly through your mouth to the count of four.
- Balanced breathing: inhale through your nose to the count of six (it can be four if six is too long or eight if it's too short) and exhale through your nose to the same count. This method of breathing is ideal when you are trying to go to sleep.
- Belly breathing: with one hand on your chest and the other on your abdomen, inhale deeply through your nose, trying to raise your diaphragm but not your chest. Do six to ten slow breaths like this or practice it for ten minutes a day. This form of breathing helps regulate the heart rate and blood pressure, and is perfect for moments of anxiety, such as before an exam. It's important not to force the belly to expand, but rather to aim for a smooth inhale and exhale cycle.

- Square breathing: inhale for four beats, hold in for four, exhale for four and count four before you repeat the process. You can add a contemplative element: for example, follow the four sides of a table or window frame (or any other square shape) with your eyes while you are breathing in this fashion. Children can be taught this method by creating a square shape on the floor with paper or tape and inviting them to slowly walk along it, while they do the breathing. You can even add a symbolic phrase to each breath, such as: "I give thanks for the air I breathe. I give thanks for the earth that holds me. I give thanks for the water I drink. I give thanks for the fire that warms me."

Advanced breathing practice

Nadi shodhana, or breathing through alternate nostrils, is part of the practice known as pranayama, or yogic breath work. It helps to focus the mind, while synchronizing brain hemispheres.

How to do it. Sitting in a comfortable meditative posture, hold your right thumb over your right nostril, and inhale deeply through your left nostril. When the inhalation reaches its peak, close your left nostril with the ring finger of your right hand, and exhale through your right nostril. Continue with the same pattern: inhaling through the right nostril, while closing the left nostril with your thumb, and then exhaling through the left nostril. It is not advisable to do this breathing practice before going to sleep as it is the yogic equivalent of an espresso coffee.

Meditating with mantras

The word "mantra" comes from Sanskrit and means a vehicle or tool for the mind. For millennia, these words or sacred sounds have been used to promote meditative states; or to generate energy, healing or spiritual growth. They are like seeds planted in the mind with a certain intention, and watered with sustained practice.

In transcendental meditation, each practitioner receives a specific mantra from her teacher. In other traditions, you are free to choose the mantra that best resonates with you, or which is the most suitable for your purpose.

The most sacred mantra of Buddhism is "Om mani padme hum," which is Sanskrit for "Oh, the jewel in the heart of the lotus!" It is the mantra of the bodhisattva Avalokiteshvara. A bodhisattva is an enlightened being who seeks collective salvation. Tibetan Buddhists consider the 14th Dalai Lama, Tenzin Gyatso, to be the current incarnation of Avalokiteshvara.

The syllable "OM" is described in the sacred Indian texts known as the Upanishads as the sound that gave rise to the universe, and which embodies the ultimate reality and the essence of life. It is, in fact, a sacred sound for four religions: Buddhism, Hinduism, Sikhism and Jainism.

One of the most revered mantras of Hinduism is "Om namah Shivaya," which means "Om! Reverences to Shiva." Shiva, together with Brahma and Vishnu, forms the Trimurti (or "three forms"), which represent the cycles of creation, conservation and destruction of the universe.

"Om shanti shanti shanti" is a mantra shared by Hinduism and Buddhism, which invokes the peace of body, speech and mind.

In ancient Christianity, the most revered mantra was "Maranatha," which in Aramaic (the language spoken by Jesus) means "Come, Lord, Come, Lord Jesus." This mantra is found in the scriptures and is one of the earliest prayers of the Christian tradition.

As well as the mantras of each tradition, it is possible to find and use a wide variety of phrases and words whose repetition evokes different moods and mental states. Here are two proposed by Vietnamese Buddhist monk and author Thich Nhat Hanh: "Present moment; wonderful moment," and "Inhaling, I calm my mind. Exhaling, I smile."

Finally, here are two mantras that are well suited to starting and ending each day. Morning mantra: "I am (inhaling), peace (exhaling)." Evening mantra: "Yes (inhaling), thank you (exhaling)."

OPEN FOCUS MEDITATION

This is a practice created by the psychologist Les Fehmi, who noted that in the Western world there is a tendency to live with a "fixed focus of attention," which is the kind of attention that the hunter uses to catch his prey: a narrow, tense, grasping gaze. Although we need fixed attention to carry out many of our daily tasks, living with this kind of attention permanently leads to unnecessary chronic stress. Fehmi teaches a simple way to counteract this tendency by adopting a relaxed, diffuse and creative form of attention, which he calls "Open Focus." Here are two ways to practice it:

Focus on a fixed point

Without moving your head or your eyes, begin to gently widen your vision to both sides, and also up and down. Once you have your widest peripheral vision, let the object of your original focus blend into the background, and make the peripheral view the foreground. Observe what happens to your breathing, your shoulders and your general muscular tension when you are on "open focus." Slowly revert to the fixed focus. Then see if you can see everything on an equal footing.

You can also practice this technique while walking: either looking ahead with open focus, or by focusing on the space in between the shapes you see, instead of on the shapes themselves (for example, the space between the branches of a tree or the space between clouds). Author Michael A. Singer calls this "a space walk." It brings a feeling of great serenity and relaxation.

Open focus meditation

Sit comfortably and close your eyes. Let your mind flutter like paper in the wind. Then see if you can successively imagine or visualize the inner space:

- between your eyes.
- between your ears.
- inside the cavity of your throat; imagine the volume of air that it contains.
- inside your ears.
- between the cavity of your throat and the cavity in your ears.

Continue in the same way, imagining the interior spaces of the rest of your body. You can also add surfaces, such as the space occupied by the palms of your hands and the soles of your feet. End with the interior space of the heart. You may visualize it as a cloud of atoms floating in the interior space of your chest, which in turn merges with the space outside your body, which stretches out in all directions, including up and down, and into infinity.

According to Fehmi, this meditation produces alpha-synchronous brain waves. In other words, the alpha waves of relaxation combined with the synchronization of both hemispheres. The sensation is as pleasant as it is unique.

MINDFULNESS, OR THE ART OF REMEMBRANCE

The term "mindfulness" is an attempt to translate the word *sati* from the original Pali, a language similar to Sanskrit, which originates from commentaries on the ancient Indian literary texts known as the Vedas. *Sati* is the noun that corresponds to the verb *sarati*: to remember.

What does the practice of mindfulness teach us to remember? Basically, to return to the present, over and over again: to come back to the here and now every time you let yourself become enveloped in thoughts of the past or future, or ruminations of any kind. And to do this with an attitude of equanimity, experiencing whatever presents itself with openness, compassion and full attentiveness. In other words, to invest mind, body and soul in whatever you are doing or feeling.

How can you practice mindfulness in every moment? By trying to remain present and attentive to whatever you are doing: when you walk, eat, meditate, talk, work or rest. Jon Kabat-Zinn, who synthesized this practice and offered it to the West, defines mindfulness as "paying intentional attention to the present moment, without judging." However, this is not as simple as it sounds; it is easy to keep forgetting to do it. It therefore requires practice. As a beginner, it is sometimes easier to experience mindfulness through physical movement. Here is one practice.

MINDFUL WALKING

Choose comfortable clothes and footwear to walk in. Begin by standing, and becoming aware of your body and how it feels. Take note of your posture; feel the weight of your body on the ground; notice all the subtle movements that keep you upright and balanced.

Allow your knees to bend slightly. Feel how your hips form the center of gravity for your entire body. Take some deep breaths from your abdomen, and bring your awareness to the present moment.

Begin to walk slowly, keeping your knees bent. With each step, notice how the heel of your foot touches the ground first, then the ball of the foot, and finally the toes; while the opposite foot rises simultaneously to take the next step.

Breathe naturally, filling your lungs completely with each inhalation, but without effort. Let your eyes focus gently on some point in front of you, while at the same time allowing yourself as much peripheral vision as possible.

When your attention drifts from the sensations of walking and breathing to chase after some thought or emotion, perceive it without judgment, and gently bring it back to the present moment.

Continue walking in this way for 5 to 20 minutes. When it is time to stop, pause and feel the body standing still again, with the ground solid beneath your feet holding it upright. Take some deep breaths.

If you like, you can end as the Buddhists do, by dedicating the merit of your practice to the well-being of all sentient beings.

Through these simple techniques, you can bring the light of consciousness to bear on your days, and learn to live gently with changing circumstances. The ever-relevant 13th-century Persian poet Rumi—a beacon of light in himself—invites us to live in equanimity in a centuries-old poem that is as timely today as many a modern psychological treatise.

The Guest House

This being human is a guest house.
Every morning a new arrival.

A joy, a depression, a meanness; some momentary awareness
comes as an unexpected visitor.

Welcome and entertain them all!
Even if they are a crowd of sorrows, who violently sweep
your house empty of its furniture,
Still, treat each guest honorably.
They may be clearing you out for some new delight.

The dark thought, shame, malice:
meet them at the door laughing and invite them in.

Be grateful for whoever comes,
because each has been sent
as a guide from beyond.

THE OCEAN
Open Your Heart

"The heart has its reasons, of which reason knows nothing at all."
Blaise Pascal

"The body is like the ocean,
rich with hidden treasures.
Open your innermost chamber
and light its lamp."
Mirabai

"With each breath, I plant the seeds of devotion.
I am a farmer of the heart."
Rumi

The breeze carries hints of salt and foam. The road has been long and our bodies yearn for the renewal promised by the sea. At last we see it. The wind swirling the waves, the distant horizon, the clouds mirrored in the water . . . the majestic, infinite ocean! All rivers converge here: the broad and the narrow; the timid and the impetuous; the ones that meander along the way, and those that come thundering home. No matter their course, their waters release here, in the vast geography of the heart.

In his autobiography, *Memories, Dreams, Reflections*, Jung tells of an encounter he had with an indigenous chief named Ochwiay Biano, or Mountain Lake. This chief of the Hopi people (one of the communities that then inhabited Taos, New Mexico) told the psychiatrist that his people were perplexed by the gaze of the white man: "Their eyes gaze so intensely, as if they are looking for something. What are they looking for? We don't know what they want, we don't understand them. We think they're crazy."

When Jung asked him what he meant by this, the man replied, "It is said they think with their heads." "And you?" Jung asked. The man pointed to his heart.

This visit led Jung to consider that cultures value thought and emotion very differently. In a letter he sent to Mountain Lake years later, the psychiatrist told him: "I am setting out to explore the truth in which the Indians believe. It has always impressed me as a great truth."

The father of depth psychology was referring to a worldview that assigns man a humble but meaningful place in the universe, and connects him with a sense of purpose. A purpose that is not so much intellectually understood as intuited; and the place where that intuition lives is the heart.

What are we talking about when we talk about the heart? We could think of it as a kind of matryoshka (Russian) doll, in which the organic functions of the heart are intertwined with other subtler, vaster and more powerful attributes.

In physiological terms, the heart is the governing organ of the body. Barely bigger than a fist, and weighing between 280 and 340 grams, it circulates oxygen and vital nutrients to all body tissues and removes carbon dioxide and other waste substances. It beats about 100,000 times per day (about 3 billion times in a lifetime), 60 to 80 times per minute, and in each cycle rests for four-tenths of a second. It is the only organ whose function includes a built-in rest period. It also produces electromagnetic waves 60 times more powerful than those of the brain. The precise effects of those waves on other people, and on the environment, are currently under study.

The heart also has an emotional dimension. *The Epic of Gilgamesh,* one of humanity's first works of literature, spoke over 3,800 years ago of the heart as "the source of our human emotions." Science today confirms that this organ is the gateway to the psycho-physiological network (also involving the brain and the nervous system) that produces the complex phenomenon we know as "the emotions."

In a spiritual sense, the heart has been identified by mystics, artists, philosophers and poets as the seat of the soul. It is here that transpersonal experiences are born and expressed. In Hinduism it is known as *anahata,* which means "the sound that does not come from any blow," or celestial sound. In Christianity, the Sacred Heart is the symbol of religious devotion. In Sufism—known as "the religion of the heart"—the heart is portrayed with wings, and it is conceived as the point of union between body, mind and spirit, as well as the temple to which one goes to pray.

It is not only sages and poets who intuitively sense that something particular happens in the center of the chest, where we feel our essence beating. We all refer to this dimension of the heart in everyday life. Our language is full of expressions that reveal that we sense this organ to be far more than enervated muscle tissue: "It broke my heart," we say, and "Listen to your heart"; "I say it from the bottom of my heart" and "I have had a change of heart." We imbue it with a special kind of intelligence, somewhere between intuition and wisdom. Surprisingly, perhaps, science today is showing that the notion of a "wise heart" is more than a metaphor.

The first scientific mention of "heart intelligence" appeared in the 1960s, when psychologists John and Beatrice Lacey conducted studies showing that the heart communicates with the brain in ways that significantly affect how we perceive and react to the events that happen to us. In 1991, the HeartMath Institute was founded in the United States, and neurocardiologist J. Andrew Armour introduced the term "heart-brain" to refer to the sophisticated nervous system with which this organ is endowed.

Over the years, HeartMath has continued to investigate the various dimensions of the heart and has come to the conclusion that it possesses a dynamic and unifying intelligence that is constantly adapting to the needs of the mind and body. It sends more signals to the brain than vice versa, and changes its rhythm according to different emotional states.

In the presence of distressing emotions, the heart rate becomes chaotic and signals are sent to the brain that inhibit cognitive function, perception, memory and the ability to make decisions. Positive emotions, on the other hand, generate a highly favorable state that HeartMath has baptized "cardiac coherence." In this state, the electromagnetic waves of the heart and the brain are synchronized; the parasympathetic nervous system is activated; the immune system is strengthened; and hormones linked to well-being are secreted. It is possible to achieve this beneficial state in minutes, by practicing simple techniques (which we will look at shortly) to invoke and radiate positive emotions.

EXPLORING EMOTIONS

In modern society, we haven't been aware of the true relevance of our emotions for long. Up until a few decades ago, they were mostly seen as a remnant of our instinctive animal nature and a hindrance to rational thinking. "Emotional illiteracy—or lack of sensitivity, understanding and savvy—has much of its rooting in the historical devaluation of emotion relative to cognition," says Robert Augustus Masters in *Emotional Intimacy: A Comprehensive Guide for Connecting with the Power of your Emotions*. Masters corrects the misunderstanding:

> Not surprisingly, research shows that the unrepressed presence of emotions significantly contributes to mental and social skills. Emotions only cloud the skies of rational thought when we lack intimacy with them. And rational thought muddies its own waters when it's cut off from emotion— slipping into, so to speak, an irrational rationality!

Today, emotions are understood as a crucial bridge between body and mind. These are only some of the functions they serve: they mediate our social bonds; direct our attention; influence memory and learning; affect judgment and cognitive processing; and guide our sense of moral discernment. We Homo sapiens not only "know that we know"—as our name indicates—we also know that we feel, and feel that we feel. We are emotionally self-aware.

All emotions—including afflictive emotions such as anger, fear, sadness, envy, jealousy, shame—play an evolutionary role.

As psychotherapist Norberto Levy states in *The Wisdom of Emotions*, afflictive emotions, far from being "negative," are highly functional alert mechanisms: they show us what is missing, or what is affecting or worrying us; and they give us the opportunity to correct it. For example, anger may tell you that something or someone has transgressed one of your boundaries. Fear warns you that you are in the presence of threat that you may not have the proper resources to face. Sadness is the awareness of a loss that demands your attention. Envy speaks of a sudden and painful perception of lack.

While these emotions are vitally important, their function is only effective if you are able to hear their message and do something to help them dissipate or transform. Conversely, if you live with them for extended periods, they can affect your health. Why? Because their emergence activates the sympathetic nervous system (the one responsible for the fight or flight response), with its consequent cascade of physiological effects: the blood drains from the cerebral cortex, clouding thoughts; the heart beats stronger; the body tightens and contracts and you isolate yourself from your environment. If you allow painful emotions to be the lens through which you look at life, your heart eventually shuts down, and the world becomes a hostile and alien place.

For much of its history, psychology was mostly concerned with studying the difficult emotions, because its main aim was to cure disorders of the psyche and to help individuals adapt better to the requirements of society. In the 1950s, humanist psychology began to turn this trend around, focusing on emotions and attitudes that don't just help people to function but to flourish. Thus began the study of "positive" emotions such as pride, satisfaction, pleasure, desire, anticipation, relief, interest, fun and euphoria. All these emotions produce pleasurable sensations and contribute to improving mood, relationships and health.

But there is a subgroup of positive emotions that are worth looking at in more detail. We will call them "essential" or "expansive" emotions, because they connect us with a dimension of existence that transcends the biological, and even the psychological, and enters the realm of the spiritual. These emotions are inherently transpersonal: they connect us with others, with nature, with the experience of the sacred, and with Love as the ultimate reality of existence.

Why Love with a capital letter? Because in addition to being an emotion, a feeling, an attitude, a decision, and a way of being and of acting, Love is also the intrinsic nature of life. There is no way to empirically demonstrate this ancient intuition—universally espoused by wisdom traditions—but it is difficult not to see it reflected in multiple mirrors, such as:

- the interdependence of all life forms, expressed even at a subatomic level;
- the impulse of all living beings to grow, prosper and interact;
- the evolution of consciousness, which every day motivates more people to cooperate to alleviate suffering and build a more compassionate world. There may be forces pushing in the opposite direction but this does not invalidate the fact that the positive tendency exists, as reflected in global statistics that reflect a reduction of violence in the world over the centuries.

Joseph Campbell, the mythologist whose voice illuminates several stages on our journey, once said that life is at once monstrous and wonderful, and we must embrace it in its wholeness. But, he added: in its center there is a sweetness. That sweetness could well be called Love.

If Love with a capital letter—Love as synonymous with consciousness—is the bottom of the ocean, from which everything emanates, we could say that actions driven by Love feed the rivers that feed the sea, from which everything is born again and again, in perpetual co-creation. Where can we see this in the journey of an individual life? In this dual movement: on the one hand, we have the commitment and the awareness of loving a person (or an idea, a cause, a place, a landscape); but if we don't feed that commitment with daily doses of loving actions, then that "love" can lose strength and luster, until it is reduced to the mere memory of something that was once there.

So what are these love-infused, transpersonal emotions that drain directly into the ocean of the heart? And what can we do to invoke them and cultivate them daily?

Emotions That Feed the Heart

Here is a list of some of the most important: wonder, awe, gratitude, joy, compassion, forgiveness, humility, kindness, hope, reverence, devotion, inspiration, contentment, humor, courage.

Because when we feel them we are close to the source, we could almost think of all these emotions as nuances or gradations of Love: each is a specific quality that arises when Love illuminates a particular facet of life. For example, awe can be thought of as the form that Love takes when it shines through the prism of mystery. You may experience it in a moment when you look up at the sky and feel your chest expand, as the Love that you are recognizes itself in the form of immensity and transcendence.

These are some of the nuances that illuminate each of the essential emotions:

Awe: love plus perception of mystery.
Joy: love plus delight.
Compassion: love plus empathy for suffering.
Gratitude: love plus perception of grace.
Appreciation: love plus recognition of virtue.
Hope: love plus a sense of meaning.
Forgiveness: love plus acceptance of fallibility.
Kindness: love plus desire for the happiness of others.
Humility: love plus transcendence of ego.
Reverence: love plus admiration.
Wonder: love plus appreciation of beauty.
Vitality: love plus vigor of body and soul.
Devotion: love plus commitment and surrender to someone or something.
Inspiration: love plus an influx of spiritual energy.
Contentment: love plus peace.
Humor: love plus appreciation of the absurd.
Courage: love plus strength and conviction.

What is the common thread that runs through all these emotions? All of them pull us out of the stuffy corners of the mind and connect us to a reality greater than our circumstances. They do not coexist for long with afflictive emotions, which are defensive by nature, but rather tend to displace them. By reminding us that we are not just our minds, bodies or stories, but part of an immeasurably greater reality, the emotions of the heart produce a strange kind of joy that cannot be fabricated by artifice nor lost by a simple change of luck.

Like fear and anger, the emotions of compassion and gratitude are rooted in the limbic brain. But, at the same time, they appear to be in a category of their own. Essential emotions seem to be the north star of evolution. They evolved later in the history of our species, and appear to be pointing the way forward. Not only do they facilitate flexible, creative, integrated and efficient thinking, and activate the parasympathetic nervous system (bringing us serenity and relaxation), but they are also the mark of emotional maturity. In childhood, youth and early adulthood, we dedicate much of our energy to developing and strengthening our ego, and defensive emotions are necessary for this process. In the second half of life, or the second adulthood, if all goes well, emotions such as anger, jealousy and envy become less frequent and intense, giving way to deeper impulses, which are closer to the heart and to our higher selves. It's not that the ego ceases to exist, by any means, but it becomes progressively subservient to the soul.

A curious fact: although all emotions are contagious by nature, essential emotions also have an "uplifting" effect: the mere fact of witnessing them, even without participating in them directly, opens the heart and expands vision. How do you feel when you see a teenager helping an old man cross the street? Or when you read about someone who puts his life in danger to save another? Or even when you watch a movie where love triumphs against all odds? How does your chest feel at such moments? What is the expression on your face? At those moments, what is your perception of the ultimate nature of life? Let's look at some of the main features of the most vital essential emotions.

Awe and wonder

Awe is the perception of something so vast—in size, quantity, dimension or quality—that it forces you to reconfigure your mental paradigms. You may be awed by a starry sky; a waterfall; a storm cloud; the moon when it rises; the sighting of a whale; a flock of geese flying in formation; a symphony; a sporting feat; or an act of supreme kindness or compassion.

The physiology of this emotion reveals something about its nature: your eyes open wide, your eyebrows arch, your chest expands. Something peculiar happens to your breathing: you inhale and hold your breath in, as if you want to make room for something so enormous that it doesn't fit into your body.

Awe reminds us of our smallness while, at the same time, making us feel connected to an immeasurable whole. Its effect is so powerful that it freezes time in the present: the moment the clouds dissipate and a majestic snowy peak appears before you, you stop thinking about the next day's tasks. People participating in scientific experiments on awe report that this emotion makes them feel serene, more aware of the time they have available to them, more appreciative of the strengths of others, more willing to give to others and more satisfied with their lives. They also experience improvements to their immune systems. Psychologists speculate that one of the direct effects of awe is to foster "prosocial" behavior: a willingness to gather and cooperate with others in our community.

There is also a different kind of awe, one which has a negative tint because it is a mixture of surprise and fear and feels like being overwhelmed. Awe in this sense is evoked by a too-close electrical storm; the vision of a tsunami; a newsreel of a Nazi rally; or by imagining yourself lost in the emptiness of space. These phenomena cause us reverential fear, because they bring us face to face with the terrifying aspect of mystery. In German theologian Rudolf Otto's terms, the *mysterium tremendum et fascinans* (the tremendous and fascinating mystery; the fact that life is at once marvelous and overwhelming). But whatever the quality of our astonishment—whether positive or negative, pleasant or terrifying—one thing is certain: we are not the same after having lived it.

ACTIVITIES TO CULTIVATE AWE

- Spend time in nature. Walk through a park. Look at the trees from below; touch their bark, admire their height, think about how old they are. Lie on your back and look at the sky, day or night. Visit a river, the sea, or any water source. Watch nature documentaries or programs about space.
- Listen to music, especially of the kind that moves you and makes you feel connected to mystery.
- Lose yourself in a work of art.
- Pay attention to small, everyday things; approach them with the inquisitiveness of a child. The Buddhist monk Thich Nhat Hanh urges us: "Drink your tea slowly and with reverence, as if it were the axis on which the world revolves—slowly, in balance, without rushing towards the future. Live the moment. Only this moment is life."

- Read or think about inspiring people. Talk to others about them.
- Remember and write about surprising facts from history, or from your personal history.
- Write about something that astonished you in the past. The emotion sparked by a memory of awe is very similar to the one felt while living through the experience in real time.
- Look for new things that surprise you: find alternate ways to go to familiar places; experiment with different ways of dressing; try music you never listen to; taste foods you have never tried before.
- Search for the unexpected in the people, landscapes and situations you know best.

Gratitude

Gratitude is the recognition of something valuable that is given to us, without us having to work for it or give anything in return. In other words, something we receive by grace alone. Regardless of whom we perceive as the giver of the gift—another person, a higher force, life itself—the emotion of gratitude emerges spontaneously inside us and moves us to do something in response: give another gift, make a gesture or express our love contained in the words "thank you." Cultivating this emotion, and the attitude that underlies it, is the only way to truly live in abundance.

"The root of joy is gratitude. It is not joy that makes us grateful, it is gratitude that gives us joy," says Brother David Steindl-Rast, a Benedictine monk of Austrian origin who is a doctor of anthropology and psychology, and author of a dozen books—and who generously wrote the preface to this book.

In *Gratefulness, the Heart of Prayer*, Brother David recalls how he discovered gratitude early in his life when he was a child in Nazi-occupied Austria. One day, he heard the air raid siren warning of an imminent strike and he ran to a nearby church and took refuge under a bench to protect himself from flying glass and falling debris. He waited for the vaulted roof of the church to collapse under the falling bombs, but this didn't happen. When the siren sounded again, announcing that the danger had passed, the boy came out. He observed:

The buildings I had seen less than an hour ago were now smoking mounds of rubble. But that there was anything at all struck me as an overwhelming surprise. My eyes fell on a few square feet of lawn in the midst of all that destruction. It was as if a friend had offered me an emerald in the hollow of his hand. Never before or after have I seen grass so surprisingly green.

That amazed boy dedicated his life to teaching others to receive the gifts that life gives us every day with awareness and genuine enthusiasm. He continues:

The moment I acknowledge the gift as gift and so acknowledge my dependence, I am free—free to go forward into full gratefulness. This fullness comes with the joy of appreciating the gift. Appreciation is a response of our feelings. Our intellect recognizes the gift as a gift, our will acknowledges it, but only our feelings respond with joy and so fully appreciate the gift.

In a video called *A Good Day* that has gone around the world several times, and to which many people turn as daily food for the spirit, Brother David invites us to live awake: "You think that this is just another day in your life. It is not just another day. It is the one day that is given to you today. It's a gift."

Even when things go wrong, says David; even when we encounter abuse, violence or injustice, we can always find an opportunity to be grateful. We can be glad to have the possibility to protest, to fight to change the way things are, or, when we can't do anything else, to learn from the experience and grow in love. "We are never more than a thought away from peace of heart," says this amazing man. How can we awaken to the unique opportunity that is each moment? Let us count the ways.

ACTIVITIES TO FOSTER GRATITUDE

- **Keep a gratitude journal.** Each morning or night, write down three different things you can be thankful for from that day. It is important to be specific (not "I give thanks for my children" but "I appreciate that my son greeted me with a smile"). You can also explain or elaborate on why you are grateful for each thing you mention. It is worth including small everyday joys such as the coffee someone made for you in the office, the sun warming you through the window or the cool breeze that wakes you up when you go out into the street.

- **Look for benefactors and find a way to thank them.** Think of people who have done something important for you in the past, and write them a thank-you letter. If possible, read it to them in person, looking them in the eyes. If they are no longer with you, you can burn the letter, bury it, or release it into a stream or river, and thus entrust it symbolically to the creative forces of the universe.

- **Stop, look, go.** This is an exercise proposed by Brother David. It is so simple that even children can learn it. What does it consist of? At any moment, no matter what is happening, you can stop (cease what you are doing so that you can be fully present), look (observe with the eyes of the heart and seek the opportunity that presents itself) and act (take the action that seems suitable for the moment: enjoy, celebrate, forgive, give thanks, or voice protest and do what is necessary to correct injustices and heal pains). "Most of the time," he says, "the opportunity that arises is to enjoy the moment."

- **Practice gratitude by omission.** When you experience an afflictive emotion, take a moment to imagine what your life would be like if you did not have all that you have—even if something is causing you stress. For example, if you have a problem with your car, remember that you are fortunate to have one. If you are arguing with someone, remember the joy of having that person as part of your life. The poet Jane Kenyon captured this feeling perfectly in her poem "Otherwise," which includes the words:

> I got out of bed
> on two strong legs.
> It might have been
> otherwise.
> I ate cereal, sweet
> milk, ripe, flawless
> peach. It might
> have been otherwise...
> ...I slept in ... a room
> with paintings on the walls,
> and planned another day
> just like this day.
> But one day, I know,
> it will be otherwise.

- **Be specific when giving thanks.** When thanking someone for something, point out the specific facts that make you feel grateful ("Thank you for serving me with a smile"). Whenever possible, offer your gratitude not only in words but with your eyes, your expression and your heart.
- **Hold the space for gratitude.** When things go wrong, and you can't find even a wisp of the emotion of gratitude in you, it can help to remember occasions when you did feel it, and make room in your heart for the possibility of the feeling coming back, which is another way of exercising hope. In this way you will create the conditions so that, when the sky clears up, you may easily find your way home. At such times you could ask for help from your friends, family or co-workers, and ask them to hold that space for you, until you can find it again for yourself.

Joy

Political feuds, economic downturns, global warming, ethnic and cultural violence, natural and personal catastrophes . . . awareness of all these ongoing troubles makes human beings a species prone to worry, discouragement, and sometimes downright alarm. The following fact, then, may come as a surprise: scientific studies show that, in the absence of stress, fear or pain, the natural state of a human being is one of calm and contentment, even joy. We are not talking here about the happiness produced by a specific event, but about that pleasure we derive by the mere fact of being alive.

You might ask: if it is such a "natural" state, why is it so easy for us to lose it? The answer is simple: evolution. For our prehistoric ancestors, adaption to the environment meant being more attentive to threats (a hovering predator, a poisonous plant, a cliff) than to sources of enjoyment. Therefore, the human brain evolved with a negative bias. Want proof? Out of the dozens of nice things you hear every day, don't you tend to focus on the one not-so-nice remark somebody uttered? This has left us with a protective and intelligent disposition, but it doesn't do much for our long-term health, much less for daily quality of life.

Various studies have found that people who report a higher frequency of joyful experiences produce more antibodies against flu and have a reduced risk of cardiovascular and lung disease, diabetes, infections and high blood pressure. They also appear to live longer than their peers.

Until recently, it was thought that our basic level of well-being was pretty much immutable. Today, especially as a result of research by psychologist

Sonja Lyubomirsky, we know that happiness is determined 50 percent by our genetic makeup, 10 percent by our circumstances and 40 percent by what we do (that is, by the attitudes and decisions we make each and every day). This is where the following practices can make a difference. You may not move from melancholy to ecstasy, but you can increase your baseline happiness in a concrete and consistent way.

ACTIVITIES TO PROMOTE JOY

- Consciously counteract the negative bias of your mind, which has a tendency to be good at learning from the bad but bad at learning from the good. The way to do this is to purposefully stop to notice positive events and take them in—really savor them, however trivial they may seem. How long should you focus on such events? Researchers recommend between 10 and 20 seconds in order to intensify the experience and give your brain a chance to record it in your medium-term memory. If you do this a dozen times a day, you will be slowly weaving a new neural network, which will make you increasingly aware of the fact that your life is already essentially joyous and fortunate.
- Share your joys with other people. Tell people about the good things that happen to you. Do things that you love to do with people you love. Joy is one of those experiences that multiply and grow when shared.
- Use your gifts and strengths. Identify your particular gifts—creativity, curiosity, altruism, social intelligence, ability to work in teams—and look for new ways to apply and expand them every day.
- Look for opportunities to give. Our brains are wired to feel pleasure in giving. Therefore, even the smallest acts of kindness produces at least as much joy for you as for the person who is on the receiving end. If you make a conscious effort to make the people around you happy through simple, everyday acts, you will be nourishing your own well-being with the best and most organic of fertilizers.

Compassion

Empathy is the ability to feel another person's emotions, and it is a founding pillar of our relationships. Compassion is the empathy we feel in the presence of another's pain, plus the desire to alleviate it. In other words, empathy plus love. All religions and wisdom traditions advocate this faculty as one of the most important to develop, and all formulate some variant of the moral precept known as the Golden Rule: "Treat others as you would want others to treat you" or, in its negative formulation: "Do not do to others what you would not want them to do to you."

It is important to differentiate between compassion and what Buddhists call its "close enemy" (a quality that resembles it but differs from it in a fundamental way): pity. It is not that it is wrong to feel pity for another person, or for a situation, but pity is a more egotistic feeling, which puts you at a distance from the pain of the other and can even (unwittingly) make you feel a bit superior for not feeling that way yourself. Compassion, on the other hand, builds a bridge, because the pain of the other hurts you as if it were your own pain, and moves you to go to their aid out of love. As an emotion, it has the capacity to draw you closer to the other while spiritually elevating both of you. Science confirms that compassion protects us whereas empathy can lead to a kind of emotional exhaustion. This is sometimes suffered by those in the caring professions and can ultimately result in burnout. With compassion, the other's pain is painful for you but your desire to help (and, very often, the chance to do so) uplifts your heart. It is what a mother feels when she puts a cold cloth on the forehead of her feverish son: there is worry in her heart, for sure, but it is surrounded and protected by a force field of love.

However, this noble impulse coexists with another evolutionary tendency in our species: that of separating people into friends and enemies, and reserving our compassion only for the former. This tendency helped protect our ancestors from succumbing to the spears of a rival clan. Today, we don't necessarily need to defend our lives at spearpoint on a daily basis, but the instinct remains.

Can you consciously expand the circle of your compassion? An experiment carried out by Tania Singer and Matthias Bolz at the Max Planck Institute in Germany confirms that you can. Researchers designed and tested a program that consisted of three stages: the sustained practice of meditation; exercises to help teach perspective-taking; and the practice of *metta*, or unconditional love (which I will explain in a moment). The subjects in the experiment spent three months on each stage and after the full nine months, different areas of the brain linked to compassion were found to have physically expanded. Clearly, with the right kind of training, we can all become more compassionate individuals.

The perspective-taking portion of this training program showed that sharpening this cognitive skill can help you soften the tendency to identify with people of the same race, religion, culture or political affiliation, and extend your circle of care and concern to all human beings; to all sentient beings; and even to the planet itself.

This doesn't mean that you have to feel personally responsible for alleviating all of the world's sorrows; only that you not remain indifferent to them, and that you are able to do your best to help whenever you can. Often, all that we can offer is a word, a hug or a silent prayer, but making even a small gesture will give you a deep and true sense of belonging.

ACTIVITIES TO FOSTER COMPASSION

- Cultivate the ability to tolerate pain—your own or someone else's—by getting in touch with your breathing and your body, and developing a sincere desire for suffering to come to an end. When someone you know is overtaken by grief or anguish, a sense of openness, acceptance and receptivity may be the greatest gift you can offer. Your response doesn't have to be perfect as long as it is sincere. Knowing that your intention is good will help you to remain open to another person whatever trials she is facing.

- Recognize the effects of compassion in your body and your soul: notice how this emotion manifests itself in your chest, throat, face; how it softens your thoughts and moderates negative emotions such as anger and frustration. Awareness of all this will enable you to contact the feeling next time you need it.

- Develop a sense of perspective. Every life contains some degree of suffering, and this fact does not make it a bad life, or one not worth living. On the contrary, says Desmond Tutu, former Archbishop of South Africa and Nobel Peace Prize laureate: "It is through weakness and vulnerability that most of us learn empathy and compassion, and discover our souls." We need to learn to trust in each other's ability to metabolize suffering and grow accordingly.

- Adopt the technique of Naikan, created in post-war Japan by a businessman named Yoshimoto Ishin. The word means "to look within." It consists of asking the following three questions about all of your relationships:

1 What did I receive from this person?
2 What did I give to her?
3 What problems and difficulties did I bring to this person's life?

Traditional Japanese culture values the role of ancestors above all else, and so you begin the practice of Naikan by thinking about your mother, in order to make you aware of the kindness shown to you by the person who raised you, however imperfect she may have been. Then, by asking the same three questions about other people who you come into contact with, you will develop a compassionate and patient attitude towards them.

- Practice compassion meditation. With your eyes closed, pay close attention to your breath and bring to mind someone you love very much. Allow yourself to feel the love this person evokes in you, and let it grow and expand. Then think about the share of suffering this person has had, and let your love flow out to her. At the same time, silently recite the following phrases: "May your suffering cease . . . May this difficult time pass . . . May things improve for you." You can extend the practice to others who are suffering, and finally send the same good wishes to all sentient beings in the world.
- Practice self-compassion. In the West, we have a marked tendency to treat ourselves badly, as if we are forever deficient in one way or another and as if nothing we do will ever be enough to make us feel worthy. Buddhist author Tara Brach calls this distorted idea of ourselves the "trance of unworthiness." Here are some practices to help counter this tendency:

1 Ask yourself, at different times of the day: Is there any part of me that I am rejecting at this moment? Just looking at that rejected aspect—tiredness, a headache, your anger, your sadness—can help you to integrate it, and to stop fighting a useless battle against yourself.
2 In moments of physical or emotional pain, you can put a hand on your heart, and say or think the following phrases, coined by self-compassion expert Kristin Neff: "This is a moment of suffering. Suffering is part of human life. Can I treat myself kindly right now?" This simple question contains much wisdom because it reminds us of three important truths: that there is nothing inherently wrong in suffering, which is an organic part of life; that we are not alone in our suffering; and that we can offer love and healing to our pain.
3 Whenever you are facing difficult emotions, such as anxiety or shame, you can practice a meditation known as RAIN, taught by Tara Brach.

These are the steps, summarized:

- **R**ecognize what is happening.
- **A**ccept that the experience is as it is.
- **I**nvestigate it with curiosity and care.
- **N**ourish yourself with self-compassion.

Here is each step in more detail:

R: Consciously admit the thoughts, feelings and behaviors that are affecting you. The first step out of the trance of unworthiness is to recognize that you are caught in a mindset of painful and limiting beliefs. You may be feeling the following "symptoms": anxiety in your body; a critical inner voice; feelings of fear, anger or shame. To begin, simply observe what is happening.

A: Accept that the experience is what it is. Accept that the thoughts, emotions and sensations you have identified are there, without trying to control, modify, evade or judge them. One way to do this is to mentally whisper "Yes" or "All is well," as a way to embrace the reality of your experience.

I: Investigate what is happening to you with interest and care. Once you accept it you can explore further, with a sense of curiosity. You may want to ask: what is most in need of attention right now? How am I experiencing this in my body? Where do I feel it exactly? What am I believing? What does this vulnerability enable me to see about myself? What do I need most? It is better to look for the answer in the body rather than in intellectual analysis.

N: Nourish yourself with self-compassion. Self-compassion emerges when you acknowledge that you are suffering, but it reaches its peak when you feed your Self with love and tenderness. You can try to find out what is most needed by that part of you that is hurt, frightened or wounded. Is it in need of a message of reassurance? Forgiveness? Companionship? Identify what gesture could provide comfort or soften your heart. It may be a mental whisper of "I'm with you"; "I'm sorry you're suffering, and I love you"; "It's not your fault"; or "Trust your generosity."

4 Geshe Thupten Jinpa, author of *A Fearless Heart: How the Courage to be Compassionate Can Transform our Lives*, recommends working on self-acceptance by remembering a person who has loved you unconditionally (perhaps your mother or father), or imagining a figure of great wisdom and compassion (such as the Buddha, who was known as "a loving friend even to a stranger" because his compassion did not depend on knowing the recipient but only on being in the presence of a sentient being). Evoke the infinite compassion of whoever you choose and direct it towards yourself. You may use phrases such as, "May your suffering cease," "May peace and calm return," "May you give yourself shelter."

5 If you hear an inner voice that invalidates you, it is important to remember that thoughts do not necessarily reflect reality. By descending from the mind to the heart, you can sometimes bypass these thoughts and connect with deeper emotions.

6 Another component of self-compassion is the ability to forgive yourself (as compassion allows us to forgive others); and it is this important feeling or act that we are going to look at now.

Forgiveness

We have all hurt and disappointed others, on purpose or without intent, just as we have all been hurt and disappointed. It is part of the human condition. The way to live with this fallibility (and its consequences) without being trapped in pain is to exercise forgiveness. Forgiveness is an action, and it is also the emotion that arises when you are able to put down the weight of your anger and reconnect with your heart. Forgiveness does not exonerate someone who has done harm; nor does it ignore the consequences of an action. Rather, it chooses to connect with something greater than the wrongdoing and the harm it may have caused.

In Buddhist psychology, forgiveness is not presented as a moral imperative, but rather as a way to end suffering and bring harmony and dignity to life. Forgiveness, seen one way, means making peace with the fact that something bad happened, and that you can do nothing to change it, although if you choose—when you are ready—you can transcend it.

Just as gratitude is more than the words "Thank you," forgiveness is not limited to the words "I forgive you." In order to be healing, an apology must be accompanied by a genuine feeling of repentance and regret. The feeling cannot be forced; it is the result of a process. If you make the attempt to forgive and cannot, perhaps the time has not yet come, and you may need to forgive yourself for that as well. If you persist, however, the emotion will most likely eventually emerge. Generosity and repetition are the two great allies of forgiveness. Here are some forgiveness meditations suggested by author and teacher Jack Kornfield.

ACTIVITIES TO CULTIVATE FORGIVENESS

- To receive forgiveness from others. There are many ways in which we can hurt, betray or abandon another, whether consciously or unconsciously, often because of pain, fear, anger or confusion. When the person you hurt is able to hear your plea for forgiveness, you may offer it directly, while offering to repair the damage that you have done, if this is possible. When this is not possible, you can still imagine that you receive forgiveness for the offence you committed. This is the meditation:

  I allow myself to remember and feel the pain I have caused others. I feel my sorrow and my regret. I feel that at last I can be free to let go of that weight, and as for forgiveness, I bring to my awareness each harm I have caused, and the people that I affected. Looking each of them in the eye, I silently say: "I ask for your forgiveness. I ask for your forgiveness."

- Forgiveness for oneself. There are many ways in which we harm, betray or abandon ourselves through words or deeds. Here is the meditation:

  I observe the ways in which I have harmed myself; I feel the weight I have been carrying as a consequence, and the possibility of releasing that weight. When you are ready, you can offer yourself forgiveness for all these faults, one by one, repeating: "For the ways in which I have caused harm to myself through action or omission, out of fear, pain or confusion, I offer myself full and heartfelt forgiveness. I forgive myself."

- Forgiveness for those who hurt us. There are many ways in which we feel we have been harmed, abused or abandoned by others, consciously or unconsciously, by word, deed or thought. This is the meditation:

I allow myself to feel the pain caused by these offenses, and I offer myself the possibility of releasing that weight by extending my forgiveness. When your heart is ready, say: "I remember now the many ways in which others have harmed and hurt me, out of fear, pain, anger and confusion. I have carried this pain in my heart for too long. To the extent that I am ready, I offer you my forgiveness. To those who have hurt me, I offer my forgiveness. I forgive them."

If you find it difficult to contact the emotion of forgiveness, you can ask either your Higher Self, a figure of wisdom and compassion, or your heart (whichever resonates most with you), for help in finding the strength to do so. You can also appeal to reason, remembering that the purpose of guilt and shame is to learn and to grow, not to embrace martyrdom.

Love

Last on our list, but first in order of importance, is the mother ship of essential emotions. Indeed, not only is it the ship but also the waves that pass over the surface of the water, the depths below, and the very ocean itself.

Although it is true that love is always with us, it is just as clear that we cannot always feel it, in the same way that music lives in all of us, but we cannot know it to be true until we open our mouths and release it as song.

The practices in "The Village" were all about how to soothe and heal the wounds that come between you and the sun that is your heart, like big black thunderclouds. The practices in this chapter invite you to go past the clouds and concentrate on amplifying the sun, through direct spiritual experience. "The moment we indulge our affections, the earth is metamorphosed, there is no winter and no night; all *ennuis* vanish, all duties even," wrote Ralph Waldo Emerson.

ACTIVITIES TO CULTIVATE LOVE

- Keep a "devotional": a notebook in which to write down phrases, ideas, quotations, thoughts, songs and memories that help you reconnect with a loving purpose. Start with inspiration to begin your day; for example:

"Wake at dawn with a winged heart and give thanks for another day of loving" (Kahlil Gibran). It is comforting to have your notebook at hand as an ever-present reminder of your true nature.

- See and be seen. Look beyond the masks people wear, their difficult emotions, their vulnerability, their wounds. Look beyond them until you see into their hearts, always yearning to love and be loved. Allow others to see the same in you.
- Practice *metta* (Pali for "universal or unconditional love"). This is one of the most transcendent meditations in Buddhism. It consists of reciting good wishes. First you direct them to yourself (since you are as deserving of love and compassion as any other person). Secondly, you send good thoughts to a benefactor (someone who has helped you or wishes you well), or to a loved one. Thirdly, you send them to a neutral person (someone you know little about and who does not evoke in you either attraction or aversion). Finally, you turn your attention to a person who you find difficult.

  You could say that the treasure of this technique is contained in the last step, since it urges you to open the doors of your heart just at the point at which you have the urge to close them. In this sense, it is a practice of equanimity and balance, and an antidote to our natural tendency to privilege a few individuals in our inner circle, and to exclude from our care and concern all those to whom we feel indifferent, or downright hostile. Even if a relationship is challenging to the point that you decide to stop seeing that person (whose attitude or behavior is causing you pain), you can still bear in mind that that person suffers and wants to be happy, just like you, and genuinely wish him happiness and an end to his suffering. Genuine good wishes may take time to emerge, but if you persist in this practice, it is likely that they will. The physical heart is a noble organ and the spiritual heart is the definition of strength and resilience.

  The wishes that you express may include:

  - May he/she be happy.
  - May he/she be in good health.
  - May he/she be safe and protected.
  - May he/she be peaceful and calm.

- Practicing centering in the heart. HeartMath has created shortcut exercises to generate this in the midst of negative emotions, or whenever you feel separate from the world. They take only a few minutes. Here are the steps:

1 Let your awareness descend from the head to the heart (as if taking an elevator down to the center of your chest).

2 Feel that you are breathing from and to that part of the body.

3 Conjure an emotion of love, appreciation, compassion or gratitude. It can help to bring to mind the image of a loved one, a place you like, or a happy memory.

4 Make a sincere effort to maintain the emotion for a period of time (if possible, 5 to 15 minutes).

5 Radiate that emotion out to the world, imagining that it reaches whoever may be in need of it.

- Good questions. Whenever you don't know how to act in a certain situation, psychologist and author Rick Hanson recommends asking questions such as: "Being a loving person, what is it important for me to do on this occasion?"; "If I trust in love, what is the right thing to do?" I'd like to add one more straightforward option: "What would love do in my place?"

For extra motivation, it may be helpful to remember the words of Albert Einstein: "A human being is part of a whole, called by us the 'Universe,' a part limited in time and space. He experiences himself, his thoughts and feelings, as something separated from the rest — a kind of optical delusion of his consciousness. This delusion is a kind of prison for us, restricting us to our personal desires and to affection for a few persons nearest us. Our task must be to free ourselves from this prison by widening our circles of compassion to embrace all living creatures and the whole of nature in its beauty."

In the final analysis, to live from the heart is not to need great things to happen in order to feel grateful, extraordinary people in order to feel love and affection, terrible events to prompt compassion, or majestic spectacles to trigger amazement. If you can make these emotions your daily bread, you will be able to bounce back from any pain, disappointment or apathy and return to that place that summons you home towards your one true north: the warm waters of the heart.

Epilogue
As It Is in Heaven

Thus we arrive at the end of a map that—like myths, like dreams—is nowhere and everywhere.

Here, where I write, it is 8 a.m. on a summer Sunday. There are hints of heat behind the breeze as I go out to receive the day. A pair of woodpeckers (brand-new parents: I have seen them with their young) feed on the ground, sheltered by the morning stillness. The parrots chat in a low tone, as if not wanting to wake anyone. The kiskadee lets out a shriek.

The elm on the corner has recovered from being pruned and is once again round, like a storybook tree. In front of the school, the pagoda tree spills its white flowers onto the sidewalk. In autumn it will give birth to pods like strings of rosary beads.

There is not a trace of the column of ants that last night dismantled the neighborhood leaf by leaf. Where did they go to collect their harvest? The swallowtail butterfly scans the garden in search of the single flower whose nectar it came into the world to sip. Her beloved (a rare orchid-like creature) plays hard to get; but she persists.

Behind the shutters some of my neighbors share their first coffee. Others drink tea alone, feasting on the silence. Many of them, I imagine, are still swimming in the waters of sleep, or slowly waking up, drenched still in adventures that in a few minutes they will barely remember, but that may, perhaps, leave a mark.

"That's the big question, the one the world throws at you every morning," says Mary Oliver: "Here you are, alive. Would you like to make a comment?"

How will you respond?

Stay in bed and savor the remnants of last night's visitations? Or go out into the world, to drink in the smells and sounds and textures of the Earth?

Perhaps you'll gather dandelion flowers that grow beside the path to add a taste of wildness to your breakfast. Maybe you'll decide to bring back leaves, seeds and pinecones, and build an altar to honor the changing scenery of the seasons on your block, in your neighborhood, in your life.

You could stop on the way to ask good questions of friends and strangers. You may be surprised by the answers that appear; especially your own.

You might choose to observe difficult emotions that rear up inside you, and surround them with the most sincere compassion you can muster. If you can't find compassion momentarily in yourself, you could borrow it from someone else.

At any time, especially at the end of the day, you may want to take a moment to give thanks for it all.

These time-honored practices, and the many others we have shared along this journey, are rites of reconnection; crumbs that we leave behind to remind ourselves that, if we get lost, home is always a simple thought or action away.

"Only that day dawns to which we are awake," said Thoreau. The man of the woods was not speaking of a once-and-for-all awakening, a clarity that descends upon us in some earth-shattering moment, banishing doubt, fear or forgetfulness forever more. No. He spoke of the kind of awakening that happens daily, every time you remember to open your eyes wide and see.

See what?

The wren, the sparrow, the thistle in the barren field, the sunflowers drinking in the light and the hailstorm pummeling the newborn buds. See your weaknesses and your daring. See the pain of your disappointment, and the joy of rediscovered hope. See the instant the world glimmers from within, and the moment it threatens to collapse. By seeing with the eyes of the heart you make life anew, and you venture out where no compass is needed, because there is no fixed destination. You go where wonder awaits.

List of Activities, Recipes & Exercises

Stage One: The Jungle

Stage Two: The Garden

Stage Three: The River

Stage Four: The Mountaintop

Stage Five: The Swamp

Bibliography

Introduction

Campbell, Joseph. *The Power of Myth*. New York: Doubleday, 1988.

Hillman, James. *The Soul's Code: In Search of Character and Calling*. New York: Warner, 1996.

Masters, Robert Augustus. *Spiritual Bypassing: When Spirituality Disconnects Us from What Really Matters*. Berkeley: North Atlantic, 2010.

Moore, Thomas. *Care of the Soul: How to add Depth and Meaning to Your Everyday Life*. London: Piatkus, 1992.

Plotkin, Bill. *Soulcraft: Crossing into the Mysteries of Nature and Psyche*. San Francisco: New World Library, 2003.

Wilber, Ken; Patten, Terry; Leonard, Adam and Morelli, Marco. *Integral Life Practice: A 21st-Century Blueprint for Physical Health, Emotional Balance, Mental Clarity and Spiritual Awakening*. Boston: Integral, 2008.

Stage One: The Jungle

Dean Moore, Kathleen. *The Pine Island Paradox*. Minneapolis: Milkweed Editions, 2014.

Gladstar, Rosemary. *Rosemary Gladstar's Medicinal Herbs: A Beginner's Guide*. North Adams: Storey, 2012.

Harrod Buhner, Stephen. *The Secret Teachings of Plants: The Intelligence of the Heart in the Direct Perception of Nature*. Rochester: Bear & Company, 2004.

Haskell, George David. *The Song of Trees: Stories from Nature's Great Connectors*. New York: Viking, 2017.

Pollan, Michael. *Second Nature. A Gardener's Education*. New York: Grove Press/Atlantic Monthly Press, 2003.

Pretor-Pinney, Gavin. *The Cloudspotter's Guide*. London: Hodder & Stoughton, 2006.

Rothenberg, David. *Why Birds Sing: A Journey into the Mysteries of Bird Song*. New York: Basic, 2005.

Thoreau, Henry David. *Walden; or, Life in the Woods*, various editions, 1854.

Wall Kimmerer, Robin. *Braiding Sweetgrass: Indigenous Wisdom, Scientific Knowledge and the Teachings of Plants*. Minneapolis: Milkweed Editions, 2014.

Weed, Susun. *Healing Wise: The Wise Woman Herbal*. Woodstock: Ash Tree Publishing, 2003.

Young, Jon. *What the Robin Knows: How Birds Reveal the Secrets of the Natural World*. Wilmington: Mariner Books, 2013.

Stage Two: The Garden

Ackerman, Diane. *A Natural History of the Senses*. New York: Vintage, 1991.

Crawford, Ilse. *The Sensual Home*. New York: Rizzoli, 1998.

Hempton, Gordon. *One Square Inch of Silence: One Man's Search for Natural Silence in a Noisy World*. New York: Atria Books, 2009.

Norris, Gunilla. *Simple Ways Towards the Sacred*. London: SPCK, 2012.

Oliver, Mary. *Long Life: Essays and Other Writings*. Cambridge, MA: Da Capo Press, 2005.

Thomsen Brits, Louisa. *The Book of Hygge: The Danish Art of Contentment, Comfort and Connection*. New York: Plume, 2017.

Wiking, Meik. *The Little Book of Hygge: The Danish Way to Live Well*. New York: Penguin Life, 2016.

Stage Three: The River

Asma, Stephen. *The Evolution of Imagination*. Chicago: University of Chicago Press, 2017.

Cameron, Julia. *The Artist's Way: A Course in Discovering and Recovering Your Creative Self*. London: Souvenir, 1994.

Cheetham, Tom. *Imaginal Love: The Meanings of Imagination in Henry Corbin and James Hillman*. London: Spring Publications, 2015.

Eliade, Mircea. *The Sacred and the Profane: the Nature of Religion*. New York: Harper Torch Books, 1959.

Fezler, William. *Imagery for Healing, Knowledge, and Power*. New York: Fireside, 1990.

Harner, Michael. *The Way of the Shaman*. New York: Harper & Row, 1980.

Johnson, Robert. *Inner Work: Using Dreams and Active Imagination for Personal Growth*. New York: HarperCollins, 1986.

Mellick, Jill. *The Art of Dreaming: Tools for Creative Dream Work*. Newburyport: Conari Press, 2001.

Stage Four: The Mountaintop

Campbell, Joseph. *The Power of Myth*. New York: Doubleday, 1988.

Jung, Carl Gustav. *Memories, Dreams, Reflections*. New York, Vintage: 1963.

Keen, Sam and Valley-Fox, Anne. *Your Mythic Journey: Finding Meaning in Your Life Through Writing and Storytelling*. New York: Penguin Putnam 1989.

Krippner, Stanley and Feinstein, David. *Personal Mythology: Using Ritual, Dreams, and Imagination to Discover Your Inner Story*. Fulton: Energy Psychology Press, 1989.

Llewellyn Vaughan-Lee. *The Return of the Feminine and the World Soul*. Salisbury, UK: The Golden Sufi Center, 2009.

Markova, Dawna. "From Rut to River: Co-Creating a Possible Future," in *The Fabric of the Future*. Newburyport: Conari Press, 1998.

Murdock, Maureen. *The Heroine's Journey*. Boston: Shambhala, 1990.

Pearson, Carol. *Awakening the Heroes Within: Twelve Archetypes to Help Us Find Ourselves and Transform the World*. San Francisco: HarperCollins, 1991.

Stage Five: The Swamp

Bly, Robert. *A Little Book on the Human Shadow*. New York: Harper-Collins, 1988.

Hollis, James. *Why Good People Do Bad Things: Understanding Our Darker Selves*. New York: Gotham, 2007.

Johnson, Robert. *Owning your Own Shadow: Understanding the Dark Side of the Psyche*. San Francisco: Harper San Francisco, 1994.

Johnson, Robert and Ruhl, Jerry. *Living your Unlived Life: Coping with Unrealized Dreams and Fulfilling your Purpose in the Second Half of Life*. New York: TarcherPerigee, 2017.

Von Franz, Marie-Louise. *Shadow and Evil in Fairy Tales*. New York: C. G. Jung Foundation Books, 1985.

Zweig, Connie and Abrams, Jeremiah (editors). *Meeting the Shadow: Hidden Power of the Dark Side of Human Nature.* New York: Penguin Putnam 1990.

Stage Six: The Village

Hollis, James. *The Eden Project: In Search of the Magical Other.* Toronto: Inner City Books, 1998.

Masters, Robert Augustus. *Emotional Intimacy: A Comprehensive Guide to Connecting with the Power of Your Emotions.* Louisville: Sounds True, 2013.

Perel, Esther. *Mating in Captivity.* New York: HarperCollins, 2006.

Schnarch, David. *Passionate Marriage: Keeping Love and Intimacy Alive in Committed Relationships.* New York: W. W. Norton & Company, 2009.

Welwood, John. *Perfect Love, Imperfect Relationships: Healing the Wound of the Heart.* Boston: Shambhala, 2006.

Winnicott, Donald. *Babies and their Mothers.* Cambridge: Perseus, 1987.

Stage Seven: The Fire

Andrae, Walter. *Die ionische Säule: Bauform oder Symbol?* Berlin: Berlin-Verlag fuer Kunstwissenschaft, 1933.

Driver, Tom. *Liberating Rites: Understanding the Transformative Power of Ritual.* Charleston: Booksearch Publishing, 2006.

Grimes, Ronald. *Deeply Into the Bone: Reinventing Rites of Passage.* Oakland: University of California Press, 2002.

Imber-Black, Evan; Roberts, Janine and Whiting, Richard. *Rituals in Families and Family Therapy.* New York: Norton, 1988.

Van Gennep, Arnold. *Rites of Passage,* (trans. Monika Vizedom and Gabriel Caffee). Chicago: University of Chicago, 1960.

Stage Eight: The Lighthouse

Dass, Ram. *Still Here: Embracing Aging, Changing, and Dying.* New York: Penguin, 2000.

Fehmi, Les. *Open Focus Brain: Harnessing the Power of Attention to Heal Mind and Body.* Durban: Trumpeter, 2008.

Kornfield, Jack. *Meditation for Beginners*. Boulder: Sounds True, 2004.

Nhat Hanh, Thich. *Being Peace*. Berkeley: Parallax Press, 1987.

Piver, Susan. *Start Here Now: An Open-Hearted Guide to the Path and Practice of Meditation*. Boulder: Shambhala, 2015.

Salzberg, Sharon. *Real Love: The Art of Mindful Connection*. New York: Flatiron Books, 2017.

Stage Nine: The Ocean

Brach, Tara. *Radical Acceptance: Awakening the Love that Heals Fear and Shame*. New York: Bantam Dell, 2003.

Jinpa, Thupten. *A Fearless Heart: How the Courage to be Compassionate Can Transform our Lives*. New York: Avery, 2015.

Jung, Carl. *Memories, Dreams, Reflections*. ibid.

Kornfield, Jack. *A Path with Heart*. New York: Bantam, 1993.

Levy, Norberto. *La sabiduría de las emociones. Cómo interpretar el miedo, el enojo, la culpa, la envidia, la vergüenza*. Buenos Aires: Debolsillo, 2003.

Masters, Robert Augustus. *Emotional Intimacy: A Comprehensive Guide to Connecting with the Power of your Emotions*. Louisville: Sounds True, 2013.

Pearsall, Paul. *The Heart's Guide*. New York: Broadway, 1998.

Acknowledgements

This book was born as a course. I shared the experience with a group of intrepid souls for the better part of a year, learning as much from them as they from me. Their courageous exploration of the different territories, and the discoveries they found along the way, is responsible for the pages you hold in your hands. My first gratitude is for them.

I would like to thank Ana Vidal, my agent, for her faith in my work, and for her help in bringing it to the English-speaking world. I lived in the United States as a teenager, and by the time we returned to Argentina, it was a cherished second home. It moves me beyond words that a small part of me will return.

Thank you, Sabine Weeke, and Findhorn Press, for welcoming my book with such generosity, and Jacqui Lewis for your artful and respectful editing of every line. My appreciation for Nick Inman for his painstaking translation, and for helping me find the equivalents of the birds and wild edibles in the northern hemisphere. What good fortune to have found a translator who shares my quirky passions!

Heartfelt gratitude for Brother David, for the priceless gift of his words, and for the delight of his friendship. And to Beto Rizzo and Lizzie Testa, wonderful souls, for introducing us, and honoring me with their affection.

I would like to recognize my friends, old and new, who inspire me and hold me up and make the world whole and true and beautiful every single day, in good times and bad.

I give my heart to my family. My father, who, upon seeing my first article in print, declared himself "president of my fan club," and remained so to the end; my mother, who became a professional woman back in the days when this wasn't the norm, and taught me to move fearlessly in the direction of my dreams; my brothers and their bright and challenging conversation; my sisters-in-law and nephews and nieces, for the sweetness of their company; my sister, who left too soon, but whose poetic voice and beauty will live with me forever.

I wish to acknowledge my family by marriage, the do Pico-Berges, for accepting me into their witty, lucid and delightful tribe. It is a joy and an honor to be able to call you my own.

My grateful tribute to Sofi and Anouk, for making me the proudest step-grandma in the universe. You are truly the gift that keeps on giving!

My devotion to Marina and Juan, for showing me ten times over what all the fuss around mothering was about, and for filling my days with joy, light and laughter.

Mauricio, all maps lead back to you. You are where wonder lives, my love.

About the Author

Photo by Alejandra López

Fabiana Fondevila is a writer, ritual maker, activist and teacher from Buenos Aires, Argentina. Her work weaves together nature exploration, dreamwork, mythic consciousness, archetypal psychology, social work and essential emotions such as awe, gratitude and aliveness. Fabiana's passion is to help bridge inner work and action in the world, so that our deepest joy and the world's needs can meet and feed each other as fully and as often as possible.

For more information visit her website: **www.fabianafondevila.com**